THE
MONEY
RULES

THE
MONEY
RULES

50 WAYS SAVVY WOMEN CAN MAKE MORE, SAVE MORE, AND HAVE MORE!

Susan Jones

Foreword by David Bach

McGraw-Hill

New York / Chicago / San Francisco / Lisbon / London
Madrid / Mexico City / Milan / New Delhi / San Juan
Seoul / Singapore / Sydney / Toronto

The McGraw·Hill Companies

1 2 3 4 5 6 7 8 9 0   DOC/DOC   0 9 8 7 6 5 4 3

ISBN 0-07-142364-8

McGraw-Hill books are available at special quantity discounts to use as premiums and sales promotions, or for use in corporate training programs. For more information, please write to the Director of Special Sales, Professional Publishing, McGraw-Hill, Two Penn Plaza, New York, NY 10121-2298. Or contact your local bookstore.

This book is printed on recycled, acid-free paper containing a minimum of 50% recycled, de-inked fiber.

To my daughters, Jordan and August,
to my dad, Jack,
and to Lekha

Contents

Contents ◄ ◄ ◄ ◄ ◄ ◄ ◄ ◄ ◄ ◄ ◄ ◄◄ ◄◄◄ ◄

NEXT, 25 DON'Ts

DOs AND DON'Ts

Foreword

Why Women and Money?

In 1993, I was hired by a major financial-services firm, which sent me to New York to be trained as a financial advisor. My class consisted of 110 men and 9 women. During our month of training, we heard from more than 200 speakers. Most of them were forgettable, but one—a woman—made a real impression on me. Her topic was demographics and why women represented the future of the investment industry. As she told it, women were closing the income gap with men, graduating from college at a faster rate than men, and starting three new businesses for every one started by a man. What's more, women controlled more than 80 percent of all purchasing decisions in America and wrote 7 out of 10 checks. She also shared some bad news—such as the fact that women in America are on average widowed at age 56, and that one in four widows are broke within 2 months of losing their husband. As a result of all this, she said, 9 out of 10 women would soon be managing their own money.

While most of the men in the class of men yawned or snickered their way through her talk, I was mesmerized. I had some personal experience with women and money. My beloved grandma Rose Bach was a self-made millionaire. She'd decided on her thirtieth birthday that she'd had her fill of being poor, and so she taught herself how to invest. Her decision to learn about money ultimately changed the destiny of our family, and she both taught and inspired my father, sister, and me to become investors.

Because of my personal connection with the subject, I took pages of notes at that lecture about women and the future of investing. When it was over, I made a point of going up and introducing myself to the speaker. I told her how moved I'd been by her message, and how I wanted to start teaching investing classes for women when I returned back home to California.

As training wrapped up, all of us in the program were called upon to get up and talk to the class about what sort of financial-advice practice we each expected to establish. Most of the men in my class shared a similar plan: I will work with high-net-worth individuals, retirees, business owners. When I shared my plan to work with women, the class snickered. A man working with women on money—even the women in the class rolled their eyes!

Fast-forward 90 days. I was preparing the agenda for my first class on women and investing. Most of my coworkers thought I was crazy. In fact, I think some of them were placing bets on how few people would show up. If so, they probably lost money, because the phone in my office soon began ringing off the hook with RSVPs from women who wanted to attend my seminar. In all, over 100 women wound up attending.

At the end of that first seminar, one of the attendees raised her hand and asked, "David, what's a good book for women about money?" Sheepishly, I admitted I didn't know, but would find out and get back to her. The next day I went to the library and to a local bookstore to do some research. To my total amazement, I discovered that the most recent book about money aimed at women was more than 20 years old!

That's when the idea for my first book, *Smart Women Finish Rich*, was born. Truth be told, if I had found a book I could have recommended to my women students and clients, I might never have written one myself. Of course, this was the mid-1990s. Today, by contrast, you can't go into a bookstore and *not* find any number of books about money for women. There are literally hundreds of them. That's the good news. The bad news is that many of them were written by people who jumped on the bandwagon after the marketplace became proven, and not all are equally valuable.

The Money Rules is *not* one of these.

Susan Jones has written a truly powerful book that can show women of any age or income level what they need to know and do now to take charge of their financial lives. Equally significant, her book also shows you what not to do! Its power comes from its simplicity. Susan's advice is solid, easy to understand, and—most important—easy to use! What's particularly wonderful about *The Money Rules* is that you don't have to read it from beginning to end. You can simply open the book anywhere and read one of the 25 "Do's" or 25 "Don'ts." You can read just one a day if you want, or read them all at once. However you decide to use this book, I know it will give you greater knowledge about your money and how it relates to your life. And with knowledge comes confidence. *The Money Rules* will give you the confidence you need to be able to use your newfound knowledge.

When Susan first sent me the manuscript, all she wanted was my feedback. I liked it so much that I volunteered to write the foreword. I've never offered to do anything like this before because I've honestly not read a book on women and money that I've enjoyed as much as this one. I'm confident you'll enjoy it too.

What's most exciting about *The Money Rules* is that I know you'll learn some things from it that can change your life for the better. (And, by the way, if you're a man reading this right now, pretend the book isn't meant just for women and read it anyway.) I promise you, it will really help you and the people you love.

Live and Finish Rich!

David Bach
New York City
Winter 2003

Introduction

This book is my collection: my collection of all the financial tidbits I wish someone had told me when I was in college, when I held my first job, when I started a business—or even years later when I hired a financial consultant.

Only no one told me.

At first, I didn't know enough to ask. Then I became so professionally successful that I was too embarrassed to admit my ignorance. So I learned by making one costly mistake after another.

Along the way, I met hundreds of women who were stumbling just as I was.

College-educated and professionally astute, these women excelled in everything except basic financial management.

But why?

My personal observation is that a number of factors have contributed to an epidemic of financial illiteracy—in every socioeconomic group of women.

First, there is an abundance of intimidating investment strategy books yet a drought of solid skills books, making it almost impossible for someone to learn the basics. Next, there is a great deal of denial about the realities of money—denial fed by the media and other cultural factors that position $1000 dresses as the "norm." Finally, many financial guides are guilt producing, leaving one to ponder a seeming state of hopelessness.

What's missing? A resource that is intellectual yet unassuming, female-friendly yet not condescending—a book that explains financial basics in real-life, appealing ways.

Money Rules is intended to be this resource: a book that is affirmative, informative, and nonthreatening. It is my intention to share this knowledge so that others may avoid the pitfalls associated with basic errors that can have profound consequences.

Take Heed

This book is not written by a financial professional. Rather, it is written by a woman who learned about money through the school of hard knocks.

While I have taken every precaution to verify points with the appropriate experts, the tips in this book remain primarily self-taught advice and are not intended to be the end-all for any particular matter—just a push in the right direction.

It goes without saying (but lawyers say that it must be said anyhow) that you should seek professional counsel whenever you find yourself in a situation that is over your head. And use your instincts to know when that point comes.

Until then, enjoy reading.

THE
MONEY
RULES

First,
25
DOs

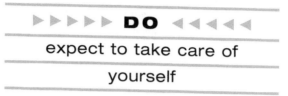

1

expect to take care of
yourself

Do you really believe that you can take care of yourself? Even more so, do you expect that you will ever really *have* to take care of yourself?

Unfortunately, many successful women harbor self-doubt, even when the evidence of their lives says otherwise. The problem is not that we can't care for ourselves. The problem is that many of us were programmed to think that we shouldn't have to take care of our financial lives and that financial success and independence will keep us from meeting the right guy. The old Cinderella theory lives today: the theory that men desire women who need to be rescued—not women who are independent and financially secure.

The root of most financial behavior is psychological, so it is critical to examine your attitudes toward money—and how those attitudes, formed early in your life, are affecting your actions today.

Think about your childhood and how you envisioned your future. Did you envision yourself in a financially lucrative career? Did you envision yourself managing your own money—or was money even a part of your self-vision?

Many of the women in my classes who have come from middle- to upper-class backgrounds have confided in me that money was just assumed in their childhoods. Even more important, in the families of these genteel women it was considered inappropriate, even rude, to ask questions about the sources or amounts of family money. Sadly, many women excel in academics and in professional careers yet fail miserably in their financial lives. Why? Because they continue to assume that money is always going to be there—and that it is rude to ask questions about money. Their privileged upbringings keep them from realizing that they must take care of themselves.

The first step toward financial success is getting a grip on your attitude toward money: why you think the way you do and how you can reprogram your attitude in order to achieve financial success. It is also letting go of your illusions about money and replacing those illusions with truth-based knowledge. A good place to start is with a financial diary. Mark a page into three columns. In the first column, record three of your activities from the past week that have involved money (e.g., shopping, saving, earning, and so on). In the second column, write down how you felt during that activity (e.g., embarrassed, proud, unsure, and so on). Then, in the third column, write how you *want* to feel the next time you engage in that activity. You will be amazed at how much self-awareness and change can come from this small exercise.

You might be surprised at the prevalence of women in difficult situations due to their lack of financial self-care. Take note of these sobering statistics:

- A quarter of all divorced women in America live at or below the poverty line.[1]
- A year after divorce, a woman's standard of living decreases anywhere from 27 to 45 percent, whereas a man's increases by an average of 10 percent.[2]
- Only 14 percent of women have $100,000 or more saved for retirement compared with 21 percent of men.[3]
- Seventy-five percent of the current elderly population are women.[4]
- Only 3 of 10 women polled have positive feelings about money.[5]

Life consists not in holding good cards but in playing those you hold well.

JOSH BILLINGS

2

understand the magic of
compound interest

Have you ever been a part of a multilevel marketing program and witnessed the power of multiples? One person tells two people, then those two people tell two each, and on and on until there are hundreds or thousands of people in the network. Well, that's how compound interest works. It is a powerful and fundamental concept for all things financial. And this is why it is important to start saving money right now even if you have never saved before and even if you can only save a small amount each month.

The magic is that over time you can accumulate more money than you actually saved; this happens because you earn interest on the money you save, and then you even earn interest on the interest. This gaining of interest on interest is called *compounding*—thus the term *compound interest*. After a period of time, the results of compound interest are astonishing—like magic.

For example, the average interest rate or rate of return paid on investments (meaning primarily stocks, bonds, and real estate) from 1990 to 2000 was 10 percent. Although stocks and other investments have taken a dive since then, it is still possible to earn 5 to 7 percent on many investments, so let's use 5 percent as an example. If you save and invest just $50 per month in a mutual fund or other interest-producing investment that would yield 5 percent growth (not a bank savings account), this means that you would invest $600 per year. If you continue to save $50 per month for 30 years, here's how your investment would look each 5 years:

After 5 years	$ 3,400
After 10 years	$ 7,750
After 15 years	$13,350
After 20 years	$20,500
After 25 years	$29,750
After 30 years	$41,600

What's the magic? The magic is that you only need to invest $18,000 in $50 increments to accumulate $41,600—so you earn a total of $23,600 from the magic of compound interest.

Another way to observe the magic is by studying the school-kid question: What would you rather have—a penny that doubles every day for 28 days or $100,000? (The answer is the penny because you will have $1,342,177.28 in 28 days.) Think about it.

So start *now*. You are worth saving for, but if it makes you feel better to save for someone else, try this:

If you have a new baby or a grandchild, try saving $100 per month in an investment account (remember that this means an investment such as a stock and not a bank savings account) from the day the child is born until he or she reaches age 6. If you never touch the money *or* add to it, and the investment earns 8 percent, your child or grandchild will be a millionaire at the age of 65, with $1,107,869 in his or her account. *All you had to invest was $7200.*

Are you convinced? The smartest move you could make today is to start saving and to invest the money in a way that will bring you the benefits of compound interest. This move is the best way to ensure a comfortable future for yourself and your loved ones.

He that fears not the future may enjoy the present.

THOMAS FULLER, M.D., GNOMOLOGIA

read the fine print

At the risk of being pedantic, I want to emphasize that this is an area where women frequently hurt themselves. In fact, the number one problem women express to me as I speak to groups about money is that they have signed agreements that they did not understand. As a result of signing such an agreement—whether it was a tax return, a lease agreement, or a marriage license—these women are paying a high price, even years later.

You just can't afford this mistake. It doesn't matter if you are single or married, with or without kids, working or at home. You have to *pay attention* to your financial affairs and to every paper you sign.

Here are the most common ways that women hurt themselves by not paying close attention:

- *Income tax returns.* Do you understand what you are signing—especially if you have no individual income but are signing a joint return? The Internal Revenue Service (IRS) will hold you responsible even if you never read the agreement. Many women spend years paying off the IRS debt of spouses because they have not paid attention to this. Even if you file separate returns, you may be liable for your spouse's debt.

- *Leases.* Are you signing a personal guarantee? This could mean that you will have to pay personally for a significant lease if your business or your spouse's or partner's business fails.

- *Mortgages.* Do you understand the points, interest rate, and prepayment penalties? Do you know your current payoff and what you have in equity? Do you know every property that your spouse owns, and are you aware of your liabilities?

- *Credit cards.* Do you understand what the interest rate, penalties, and membership fees will be after the introductory offer expires? Are you aware of how much interest you are currently paying? Do you have joint accounts with your spouse, and if so, are you sure that the joint accounts are being paid promptly?

- *Investment or banking accounts.* Are you checking the monthly activity statements to make sure that there are no errors? It is *your* responsibility—not the financial institution's—to check for accuracy.

It is mandatory to read and understand any document that pertains to your personal finances (which means any document), and no one will accept the "I didn't have time" excuse.

So make time. Women historically have been too trusting of other people's advice for their financial affairs and have given in to the ages-old "you'll be fine" counsel.

The truth is that *you will only be fine* if you truly understand the ramifications of everything you sign.

So what do you do if you are under pressure to sign a document and yet you are unsure of its implications?

Here are some suggestions:

1. Realize that *every* document has financial implications—even if the document is not specifically financial.
2. Never let someone press you into signing a document you do not understand. It is always better to wait than to sign something you will regret later.
3. When in doubt, call in an expert. The money for professional legal and/or financial advice will be well spent, and even if the professional expense seems frivolous at the time, the counsel may save you significant amounts of money later. If you are not completely satisfied with the advice you are given the first time, seek additional counsel until you are satisfied.
4. Never let someone intimidate you into thinking that any question you ask about a document is superfluous, stupid, or a waste of time.

Remember that it is possible for one signature to have a lifetime of consequences. Make sure that you understand each and every possible consequence and weigh your decisions carefully before you sign.

You will never "find" time for anything. If you want time you must make it.

CHARLES BUXTON

4

I understand.

In my dealings with women in all socioeconomic groups, I have found that a reluctance to really dig in and manage one's money is a common denominator among well-educated women in very sophisticated circumstances and less-educated women in less sophisticated surroundings. It is not that either group of women is incapable of making or handling money wisely—it is just that money, for a variety of psychological reasons, has become something negative: a bother—a thing for someone else to handle. In fact, I have been surprised that a reluctance to handle money and a resulting ignorance seem to be more prevalent in higher-end demographics. (My suspicion is that women in higher income brackets, whether the income is self-made, inherited, or from a spouse, have the opportunity to live the illusion that things are OK, whereas women with less money have to face the facts more quickly.)

As a result of this reluctance to handle money, women frequently view financial management as a chore and look for someone else to take over. Sometimes the takeover person is a husband. Other times the person is a business associate or even a financial professional. But guess what? *No one* cares about your money as much as you do—no matter how great the takeover person's credentials might seem.

Here's a way to put the importance of financial self-management in perspective:

Many of us can remember a time when a women would visit a doctor to examine a breast lump and then simply take the doctor's word that "everything is OK." But how many of us would react so complacently now? I don't know one woman today who would take "OK" for an answer when it comes to a health crisis and possible breast cancer. However, the same women who boldly question doctors and get second opinions about health issues are often still complacent about their financial health, the consequences of which can be every bit as deadly as cancer.

So here is the message: Handle your financial self with the same care you would give to your physical self.

For example, if you have an intuition that something is wrong with your physical body, you naturally listen to that intuition and seek help. If you go to a doctor and you don't feel quite right about the advice you are getting, you ask questions, and you may even get a second opinion. You read up on the issue, and you ask other women what they think.

This is *exactly* what you need to do to take care of your financial health:

1. *Listen to your intuition.* Is something inside you worried about debt, a salary issue, your spouse's money manage-

ment, or the financial advice you are getting? Listen to your intuition, and write down your concerns. Be as specific as you can. Most of all, be real with yourself.

2. *Talk with your friends.* Tell them your honest concerns, and see if they have experience or resources to share. You may be surprised at their ability to help and empathize.

3. *Ask questions.* If something is bothering you about a financial advisor's counsel, call that advisor and ask to have coffee. (This is less adversarial and sets an open tone.) Take your list of concerns, and be prepared to ask questions about specific things. *Never* let anyone intimidate you into thinking that your questions are stupid or insignificant. If you are concerned about the financial information you are hearing from a spouse or business associate, plan a meeting with a third-party counselor to address your concerns.

4. *Keep asking questions.* Don't stop until you are completely comfortable that all your concerns have been addressed. In addition, keep asking questions on a regular basis—just as you would go to your doctor for a health checkup, go to your financial advisors (friends of professionals) for regular financial checkups.

Need some encouragement? Well, just as women are faring better health-wise due to increased self-care, women who take action financially are also moving ahead.

A study of more than 35,000 discount brokerage customers at the University of California between 1991 and 1997 found that women's portfolios earned, on average, 1.4 percentage points more a year than men's did. In addition, single women fared even better than their married counterparts— earning 2.3 percentage points more per year.[6]

The message? You, as a woman, have the instincts, intelligence, and networking abilities to be a natural winner financially. You are already using these take-charge talents in the work arena and in the medical arena. All it takes now is applying that same confidence to look honestly at yourself and to act with conviction in the financial arena—conviction and courage based on the knowledge that your financial health is just as important as your physical health.

Life shrinks or expands in proportion to one's courage.

ANAIS NIN

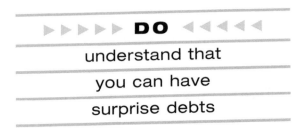

5

▶ ▶ ▶ ▶ ▶ **DO** ◀ ◀ ◀ ◀ ◀

understand that
you can have
surprise debts

If any of the following sounds like it might apply to you, then pay close attention and think seriously about seeking legal counsel. The issue of surprise debts can be quite complicated—especially in community-property states, of which there are nine: Arizona, California, Idaho, Louisiana, Texas, New Mexico, Nevada, Washington, and Wisconsin. (All other states are called *common-law states* and treat marriage income somewhat differently.)

Many women have found themselves in ugly predicaments because they didn't have a clue about the debts they had incurred due to another person's actions. And yes, you can be in debt and not even know it.

Here are some of the most common debts that can sneak up and surprise you:

- If you are married and live in a community-property state such as Texas, you are not only the recipient of half your spouse's earnings, you are also the recipient of half the personal debt he accumulates, with or without your knowledge, during your marriage. This means that if your

spouse obligates himself for a business or personal debt—
say, he buys a boat or invests in a company—you are most
likely responsible for half the debt—*even if you had no
knowledge* of the debt and would have never agreed to it.

- You may owe one-half the debt your spouse has personally guaranteed, such as office or equipment leases. This
is true even if you did not know about the obligation and
did not sign in approval.

- You may be responsible for one-half of any Internal
Revenue Service (IRS) obligations while you are married,
even if you did not participate in the actions that caused
the debt and/or were "ignorant" of the circumstances.
Ignorance is not an excuse with the IRS, although the IRS
has established a more favorable "innocent spouse"
viewpoint.

- You may have liability if you serve on a board of direc-
tors and the organization is ever sued (this is true even for
nonprofits such as schools).

- If you have minor children and they have credit cards,
this means that you have given *implicit* approval for their
charges—knowingly or not. If your kids cannot pay, you
may be liable for the charges.

- If you are in an automobile accident and the injuries
exceed the limits of your policy, you can be sued for
damages. The same is true for homeowner's insurance
and accidents.

- If you are divorced, you still may be liable for joint
accounts. You must actively close these or ask in writing
to be removed from the account.

Many women have been shocked to find that their personal fortunes and earnings have gone down the drain to pay for a spouse's debt, about which they had no knowledge.

It is critical to understand the financial assets and debts of anyone with whom you are in a partnership—whether the partnership is business or personal. Knowledge is the first step. But the second step is equally important because there are ways to protect yourself from virtually every situation. These solutions include setting up corporations to contain debt and protect personal assets, prenuptial agreements to define liability and asset distribution, and legal agreements and insurance to protect you from possible lawsuits.

Hope for the best, prepare for the worst, and shoot down the middle.

PRAGMATIC CREED

6

Are you in love? Then now is the perfect time to make sure that future financial issues do not get in the way of your relationship. A prenuptial agreement is not a slap in Cupid's face—it is an acknowledgment that both you and your partner are looking out for your best individual and collective interests. In my experience, most women fear prenuptial agreements and believe that they always give the man the upper hand. But this is not true.

A good prenuptial agreement protects you as much as it protects him. In fact, in my classes I have seen more women hurt by the lack of a prenuptial agreement than men. Among other things, a prenuptial agreement will protect you from being treated as a "nonfinancial contributor" if you are a stay-at-home wife and later face a divorce and alimony negotiations; it will provide a platform for stating shared goals and expectations; and it will protect you from any negative backlog from your spouse's business dealings.

In particular, prenuptial agreements are important for anyone with assets to protect, for women going into second marriages, and for women going into first marriages with men who have been married previously. A prenuptial agreement also can provide important legal separation from your husband's business entities (read *debt*) and set forth division of economic and family responsibilities. An all too common scenario is the woman who gives her life savings to help her husband start a new business venture—and then watches as the business venture, the money, and the love disappear.

Here's a hint from a leading divorce attorney: Don't wait until the last minute when you are frazzled with wedding details to do this prenuptial agreement. Consult with an attorney, mull it over, and finalize your agreement well before the wedding day so that there is no possibility that you will succumb to pressure on issues about which there may be disagreement.

Even in community-property states, a court does not have to divide property in half in the case of divorce. Considerations such as cruelty and adultery may change a judge's mind. Still, the best practice is to go into any marriage knowing just how a divorce would affect you financially. It is also critical that you always keep enough money in your own name to enable you to leave, if it is suddenly necessary, and to stand on your own two feet.

While you may not want to think about divorce while you are planning a wedding, the statistics suggest that it is foolishness not to. The national divorce rate is 54 percent,[7] so it's a good idea to think about the what-ifs before they happen.

He that gives his heart will not deny his money.

THOMAS FULLER, M.D.

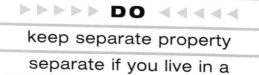

▷ ▷ ▷ ▷ ▷ **DO** ◁ ◁ ◁ ◁ ◁

keep separate property separate if you live in a community-property state

If you live in a community-property state, it is critical for you to understand the difference in community and separate property. *Separate property* is any money or assets of value (such as real estate) that you owned prior to your marriage and keep separate after your marriage. It's also one-half of what you earn during your marriage—if the funds are kept separate. *Community property* is anything that you earn or gain (assets and liabilities) in any way during your marriage, and it is one-half yours and one-half his.*

The problem is that most women don't understand why or how to keep property separate. Here's a crash course (but see a lawyer if you are about to tie or untie the knot—this is important for your prenuptial agreement.

WHY KEEP YOUR MONEY SEPARATE

- You need money that is clearly yours should you ever divorce in an unpleasant way and find yourself without spousal support—or if you just need funds of your own

*Community-property states are Arizona, California, Idaho, Louisiana, Texas, New Mexico, Nevada, Washington, and Wisconsin.

that your spouse cannot touch for any type of emergency purpose.

- Any money that is commingled (meaning, put in the same account) with your husband's money can never again be counted as separate property—even if it was inherited from your family. This means that if, for example, your husband has a debt that he cannot pay—the person/company he is indebted to may access your personal funds to pay this debt *if* your funds have not been kept separate. It does not matter if the money was left to you by your great-grandmother and you never had any intention of touching it—it is touchable once you comingle the money with your spouse's.

- In a community-property state, every penny or other asset owned by a couple is legally one-half yours and one-half his. That is true whether or not you or he works.

How to Keep Money Separate

- When you marry or if you receive inheritance monies, place your money in an account labeled with your name and the specific words "Separate Property." Any bank or investment institution can do this. Never put money from your husband in this account, and don't put his or your future earnings there either.

- When you receive earned income (yours or his), put one-half of it in your account and one-half in his. Of course, this can be touchy, and this is why discussing money before you marry and signing a prenuptial agreement are in your best interest.

- Consider a joint account for household expenses, and develop a budget for deposits and withdrawals. This would mean, of course, that you and your spouse would take equal portions from your separate accounts and put the funds in the joint account where they may be accessed by you both.

Many women feel that it is selfish to put away money for themselves, but many more women have learned the hard way that this is important. No matter how wonderful your marriage, you need to be able to live independently if circumstances of any sort should necessitate such a move.

Taking care of yourself is not selfish. It is healthy.

I don't care too much for money. Money can't buy me love.

PAUL McCARTNEY

8

check your credit report

once a year

When was the last time you checked your credit report? Do you even know that you have a credit report?

A credit report is a summary of your financial life—what you owe now, what you owed in the past, what you have paid, and what you are still paying. It shows what bills have been paid on time and when you have been late paying. It's like a school report card—except this report grades your financial life. There are three companies in the United States that keep track of all this information: TransUnion LLC, Experian, and Equifax. (Additional information is available in the Resources section of this book.)

When you apply for any type of loan—car, home, credit card—you are implicitly allowing the company with whom you are applying to check your credit report. Potential employers, insurance issuers, and landlords also may check your credit report if you provide your Social Security Number.

Unfortunately, the information on your credit report probably is not totally accurate and will affect your "image" negatively. A very bad report will make it impossible for you to get a loan or even a job, whereas a slightly bad report will cause the lender to charge you a higher interest rate. This is so because the people who construct loans and leases look at your credit report to predict whether or not you are a good risk; in other words, they use your past payment behavior to predict your future behavior and will charge you less interest if they believe you will pay the loan or lease fully and on time.

Employers and all types of insurance issuers (automobile, home, health, and life) are also increasingly looking at credit reports before making hiring and policy rate decisions because they believe that financial responsibility is an indicator of overall responsibility. In fact, 92 percent of all auto insurance companies and 90 percent of property insurers are now using credit scores to determine insurance rates, and almost all employers and landlords take a look at credit reports before hiring.

Many people think that they can overcome a few delinquent payments by showing a high income, but my contacts in the mortgage business tell me that high income is *no indication* of a good credit report. In fact, many of the credit problems mortgage bankers see are the result of overly busy doctors or executives who mistakenly think that their incomes will make up for "trivial" mistakes. However, income is only one factor when someone is looking at you from a creditworthy perspective. You are also being examined to see if you paid that $50 department store bill on time 3 years ago, so pay attention to the details.

Here's how it works. When you apply for a significant loan, the first thing the lender will do is look at your credit history. The most current history (the last year) contains the most important data. And big things such as timely payments on cars, homes, and credit cards are most important. But small things have an impact too, although they are usually easy to remedy.

For example, you may have turned in your cable box but not received proper credit from the cable company. This counts, and it is not the cable company's problem to fix—it's yours. What do you do? You contact the cable company and ask for a written document stating that *you* and not the cable company has canceled your service. Then you send a copy of that document to each of the three credit reporting agencies. Also, those overdue medical bills that you are waiting for the insurance company to pay? Well, a letter to the credit agencies explaining these bills and the fact that you are awaiting insurance funds is all that is needed.

So what do you do? The first thing you need to do is to take responsibility for your credit report. It is possible to find out what is on the report and to change the information. You can change inaccuracies, dispute information, and even add comments to areas that need a special explanation.

Here's how:

1. *Write and ask for your credit report* (or request a copy online). See the Resources section in this book for details.

2. *Ask the reporting company to include a Beacon or FICO score.* This is the total score that is always sent to inquiring lenders but often not to consumers.

3. *Understand your scores.* In general, Beacon and FICO scores must be above 620 for you to qualify for a favorable interest rate. If your score is below 620, you will be

offered a higher interest rate, as well as possible negative impressions from insurance companies, leasing agents, and even employers.

4. *Take action to clean up any inaccuracies on your report.* (Again, look at the Resources section in this book and also at Don't number 7 for more information on this topic.) Clear your report of inaccuracies. This has to be done by writing each of the individual credit bureaus and providing proof of the error. If needed, contact a credit counselor to help you to accomplish this. The National Foundation for Credit Counseling is a place to start (www.nfcc.org). Keep every letter you write regarding your report because you may need it to show your lender. It takes 3 to 6 months to effect any change on a report, so until then, your best defense is a folder of documents detailing the errors. Lenders *will* consider these documents as valid.

5. *Vow to always make payments on time.* Ask every lender to tell you at what point they mark you late to the credit agencies. Sometimes this is after 30 days, yet sometimes it is after 60 days, so it is critical to know and keep ahead of this curve. It is important to keep a record of all payments too so that you have proof if needed.

6. *Limit any new credit, and do not allow car salespeople, stores, or other loan organizations to access your credit report.* Just do not give them your Social Security Number. Why? Because new inquiries, even if they do not result in increased credit, do lower your credit scores. This is so because lenders assume that if you are shopping around, you are spending money.

7. *Keep checking your report—at least yearly—to ensure that it is accurate and reflects the positive changes you are making.*

8. *Understand what credit scores mean to you.*

The following example shows what happens if you borrow $100,000 over 30 years. The better your credit score, the lower your interest payment will be—meaning that you have more money for other things.

- $267,375 will be paid at 8 percent.
- $287,481 will be paid at 9 percent.
- $313,293 will be paid at 10 percent.
- $366,620 will be paid at 12 percent.
- $421,626 will be paid at 14 percent.

Bottom line? Using the preceding example, a person with a less than great credit report will pay $154,251 *more* in interest on $100,000 borrowed over 30 years than someone with a great credit report. This is a substantial amount.

It may help to think about your credit report in this way: It isn't something that costs you money—it is something that can *save* you money in needless interest charges over your lifetime—money that is sizable enough to fund a child's education or your retirement.

Taking the time to pay close attention will yield enormous rewards.

Money often costs too much.

RALPH WALDO EMERSON

9

make one or two extra
house payments each year

This is one thing I especially regret not knowing—but don't expect your home mortgage company to tell you. Just like the credit-card companies, mortgage companies make more money if you take your time paying.

Most of us have 30-year mortgages and make monthly payments for our homes. But you don't *have* to take 30 years to pay off your mortgage. You can pay it more quickly and in the process save a great deal of money. I am not suggesting that you rework your home loan to force you into a shorter payout—this may put too much financial strain on you and cause you to use high-rate credit cards, which would defeat the purpose.

Instead, I am suggesting that you make one or two extra payments each year, if you possibly can. But first be certain that you do not have a prepayment penalty on your home mortgage. In order to determine this, you have to look at your original mortgage documents. If you are not sure, call your mortgage company. If you already have a loan and it does contain a prepayment clause, then try to refinance and obtain a loan without this. If you are in the process of buying or refinancing, make sure that a prepayment clause is not included.

A prepayment clause makes it expensive to pay your home off early and is absolutely unnecessary. However, don't expect your lender or realtor to warn you about this. The mortgage companies make more money if you don't see this clause and take a full 30 years to pay, so it's up to you to be the sleuth.

Presuming that you have no prepayment penalty, here's why you should make additional mortgage payments:

- No matter what your home value or interest rate, if you make one extra payment per year, you will reduce the number of years on your mortgage from 30 to approximately 24 years. This translates to a savings of $29,018 for a $100,000 mortgage financed at 6.5 percent.
- If you make two extra payments per year, you will reduce the number of years from 30 to approximately 20. This translates into a savings of $46,158 for a $100,000 mortgage financed at 6.5 percent.

Who wouldn't want to save this money—and how easy it is for most of us to do this—if we only understand the significance.

Also, home refinancing is a big trend now and *may* be something important for you. But beware of adding years just to get a lower interest rate. Be sure to look at the long-term investment cost and make a prudent decision before refinancing.

That man is the richest whose pleasures are the cheapest.

Henry David Thoreau

10

insure yourself

If you are a mom—working or stay-at-home—you need to have life insurance. Yet many women expect that their husbands will take care of the insurance—and that it is somehow selfish or even macabre to buy life insurance for oneself.

If you think this way, think again.

We've all had friends die unexpectedly, leaving behind a husband and two kids who now need to replace the mom with a driver, cook, maid, tutor, psychologist, and who knows what else.

While at one time it may have been traditional for the husband to insure the wife, things have since changed. The facts are that men are less likely to insure women than the other way around. Therefore, to make sure that your kids don't endure financial stress on top of everything else if you were gone, make sure that *you* are insured properly.

As a rule of thumb, you need a minimum of 8 to 10 times your annual income in life insurance. But think more in terms of 15 percent if you anticipate college or other significant costs. The *minimum* life insurance you should have is 6 times your annual income.

When you are purchasing life insurance, it's a good idea to consult with an independent broker rather than a specific insurance company because you will be offered more choices. It's also important to ask your broker if there is a guaranteed renewal at a level rate at the end of the policy term. You want to make sure that there is—otherwise, you may be forfeiting long-term value for short-term discounts. (Also be aware that most brokers earn as much as 80 percent in first-year commissions on the sale of a policy—so don't be afraid to use their time and ask questions until you are satisfied that you have the right policy.) However, it's a good idea to check the Internet for rates first; try insurance.com, quotesmith.com, or quicken.com.

It is universally felt by professionals in the insurance arena that women dramatically undervalue the stay-at-home role and therefore unintentionally put their families at risk by not having sufficient life insurance. In addition, you should consider disability insurance; we are all more likely to need this than life insurance.

Why worry about disability insurance? Because the facts are that you are more likely to become disabled than to die;[8] an astonishing one out of eight people will suffer a serious disability during their work lives, whereas far fewer will actually die. In addition, disability insurance is very difficult to get if you wait until you need it, so purchase it while you are healthy. The benefits generally provide 60 percent of your income (tax-free if you are paying for it yourself).

Unfortunately, many people underestimate what they need in terms of both life and disability insurance. A recent study by The Hartford Financial Services Group, Inc., found that 64.6 percent of all respondents with incomes in excess of $100,000 per year had less than $500,000 in coverage.[9] Unfortunately, this amount is not enough to permanently replace one's salary, and yet the respondents felt that they were insured properly.

The same survey found that 38 percent of the emerging affluent population did not review their life insurance coverage after a major life event, and 67 percent said that they did not review their coverage annually.

The surprising news is that people with higher incomes often are underinsured and overexposed. The good news is that you can take action now and make sure that you are insured properly.

Money isn't everything as long as you have enough.

MALCOLM FORBES

11

make sure your
spouse is insured

Caution: You may assume that your high-earning husband has enough life insurance to care for you and the kids if he dies, but the reality is that lots of men don't. Some men prefer to live in denial, thinking that they will never die or that they will make millions before they die and won't need insurance.

So don't wait for him. Yes, he'll know—most policies require some type of medical exam, so you can't secretly insure him—but it's worth a fight if necessary to obtain peace of mind. Pay for his insurance yourself if necessary. Make sure that your spouse has at least 8 to 10 times his annual income in life insurance, but consider more depending on your life circumstances. Think about what you would need to live if your spouse were to die. Obviously, children, college tuitions, home mortgages, and other financial responsibilities vary, so buying insurance is an individual process. Keep in mind that you usually need more than you think.

Also take note of disability insurance, and make sure that your spouse has this insurance. Many large corporations cover disability, but some have cut back benefits recently, so don't assume anything. If your spouse does not have disability insurance, then encourage him to get it. The likelihood of him dying is much less than the likelihood of him being disabled, and the financial strain of disability can be catastrophic. Your husband's disability would require you to care for him without an income stream. So pay for his disability insurance yourself if he won't pay for it.

For both you and your spouse, you have the option of buying term or cash-value insurance, which comes in two types called *whole life* and *universal life*. These types of insurance are often confused. But you can remember the meaning of term insurance by its name: Term insurance covers you for a term, or period of years. A cash-value policy covers you for life and has a cash value, meaning that the insurance company puts your premium payments, minus their fees, into a savings account.

Here is the big difference between these two types of policies: Term life insurance costs less because when your policy expires at the end of your term, you have no cash value; in other words, you don't get any money back just because you lived. In this case, the insurance company is betting on the probability that you will not die during your "term" with them, so this insurance is less costly than whole life. Whole life insurance provides cash value because you are paying more to have coverage for your entire life, and of course, the insurance company knows that we all die at some point and therefore that it will have to pay up. Universal life insurance is similar to whole life insurance except that it provides a possibly higher rate of return. However, since rates of return are projected and not guaranteed, it is usually not the first choice in life insurance options.

Generally speaking, it is wise to buy term life insurance and disability insurance. These are the two musts, yet many people avoid doing this, putting off decisions until another day. In fact, nearly 41 percent of people in a study by The Hartford Financial Services Group, Inc., indicated that they had difficulty understanding their coverage and didn't know whether it was adequate. The top two reasons given were complexity of the policies and unclear language.[10] Unfortunately, the insurers don't make it easy to understand, so here again, it's up to you to stop and ask the questions you need to ask before making any insurance decisions.

It may go without saying, but be sure that you understand just exactly whom is named as the beneficiary of your spouse's life insurance. Many second and third wives have *assumed* that their husbands have taken former wives off the policy, but often this is not the case. If your husband has not specifically changed his policy to name you as the beneficiary of his life insurance policy, you will be left high and dry at the time of his death—no matter how much he may have loved you or how long you were married. On the other hand, if you are a first wife, you need to protect the life insurance benefits for your dependent children. If you divorce and your ex-husband remarries, make sure that some of the insurance benefits remain for your children.

So don't assume anything. Ask your spouse for a copy of all his insurance policies, and make sure that you understand the coverage.

Be not penny-wise: riches have wings, and sometimes they fly away of themselves; sometimes they must be set flying to bring in more.

FRANCIS BACON

12

No matter what sacrifices it may require—never, ever earn an income without saving at least 5 percent (more if at all possible) of your before-tax dollars. It doesn't matter how tight your budget is—it will never get easier if you don't start to save now. It's that simple and that important because small amounts of savings now can ensure that you'll be sitting pretty in your later years.

Now where do you put that savings? Your strategy for *where* is just as important as your strategy for *how much*.

Here's what to do:

1. *If you are employed, save first in your company's retirement account, often called a 401(k), which is tax-deferred.* This means that you do not pay taxes on the money you put into this account until you withdraw funds, and the account is set up so that you pay a penalty if you withdraw funds before retirement. Many employers offer matching funds, yet human resources executives say that many women in top jobs often fail to sign up for this important benefit. This is unwise because the money you save in this account will not be taxed unless you withdraw it prematurely, which is considered to be before

the age of 59½. If you are confused about how to sign up for your company's retirement plan, go privately to your human resources person and talk to him or her. Make sure that you save the maximum amount allowed, which in 2003 is $12,000 unless you are 50 years of age or older, and then the maximum amount allowed is $14,000.

2. *Ask questions about how your company's retirement savings plan is structured, and recognize that you do have options.* In other words, you are allowed to give instructions regarding how the money you save in this account will be invested. It is generally unwise (think Enron) to put everything in company stock. A good rule of thumb is to allow no more than 25 percent of your savings to be invested in your company's stock.

3. *When you leave a company, take your money with you via an Individual Retirement Account (IRA) rollover, which is a way to move the money from your former company's retirement plan to another tax-deferred plan.* If you just withdraw your 401(k) money and put it in your personal account, you will pay taxes and penalties, so this is unwise. Although most companies allow you to retain your 401(k) with them, it is better for your money to travel with you to your next job so that you can keep an eye on things more easily. If you do withdraw your 401(k) funds yourself, you will have 60 days to get them into a rollover account without suffering a penalty.

4. *In addition to saving in a 401(k) company program, save at least 3 months of living expenses in an interest-bearing*

bank account. You will not receive much interest—maybe 1 to 2 percent—but this is your emergency account and must not be touched unless you lose your job or have an illness. These emergency funds are best put in a liquid account such as a money market or savings account with both your name and your spouse's name on the account for easy access in case of a crisis.

5. *If you are self-employed and not incorporated, you can fund your retirement in a tax-deferred account called a Simplified Employee Pension Individual Retirement Account (SEP IRA) or Keogh plan, which are both similar to the corporate 401(k).* These plans offer tax-deferred savings so that you can invest for your retirement. In a SEP IRA, you usually can contribute up to 15 percent of your net income, but your contribution cannot exceed $30,000. A Keogh plan is more complicated and demands more responsibility if you employ anyone.

6. *Remember that it will take approximately 80 percent of what you currently make to fund your retirement, and Social Security pays a maximum of about $1200 per month—if you have been a high wage earner.*

The rest is up to you, so funding your future is critical.

My problem lies in reconciling my gross habits with my net income.

ERROL FLYNN

13

If you work for someone else, you probably have the opportunity to invest in the company's 401(k) plan. If you are self-employed, there are ways to set up your own version of a tax-deferred account, but you will need professional advice.

Despite all the recent problems with big, publicly traded companies, assets in 401(k) savings plans overall have not dropped as much as the stock market because generally companies invest their employees' 401(k) monies in very secure and diversified investments.

Why is a 401(k) so important? The big reason is that a 401(k) allows you to save a percentage of the money you earn *before* it is taxed. This is a major advantage because you save hard cash—the percentage that would otherwise be taxed. Another advantage is that the funds typically are invested in what is called a *diverse portfolio* (which means not having all your eggs in one basket), so it's safer than investing on your own.

Finally, it's good to save in a 401(k) because there are lots of penalties for withdrawing your funds before retirement. The penalties are positive because they mean that you will be less likely to spend this money and more likely to keep it in savings. Yes, you can borrow against your 401(k), but even that requires some work, so it's not as though you can spot a new car, withdraw the cash, and speed down the road.

Assuming that you have a 401(k), I plead with you to understand it. Go to enrollment meetings and ask questions. Read your monthly statements. Understand that this is your money and that it is your responsibility to make sure that it is well managed. To learn more about basic 401(k) principles, go to www.401k-site.com. This site is helpful for both employers and employees.

Also understand that there is a limit on 401(k) contributions. The current limit (2003) is $12,000. If you are over age 50, you often can put away an additional $2000 to help you catch up on contributions.

If your company does not offer a 401(k) or you are self-employed, then you must set up your own Individual Retirement Account (IRA). This is a way for you to have the advantages of tax-exempt savings without your company's support. The two main options are the Simplified Employee Pension Individual Retirement Account (SEP IRA) and the Keogh plan. The SEP IRA allows you to contribute up to 15 percent of your income, whereas the Keogh plan allows you to contribute more. Both the SEP IRA and the Keogh plan limit your contributions to a maximum of $30,000. There are other options as well, so before you make a decision, check out www.investsafe.com.

After you've done your research, it is advisable to get professional assistance to set up your IRA.

Think about this: If you start contributing the minimum amount to your 401(k) at age 25 and continue this throughout your career, you will almost certainly be a millionaire by age 65. If you are 40 or over and just starting (and many people are), don't think it is too late. You will still benefit from this miracle of tax-deferred savings.

The only way to predict the future is to have power to shape the future.

ERIC HOFFER

14

learn to invest

Investments are anything you do with your money to make more money. And some investments obviously are more secure than others. If you are just starting out, here are some tips.

While it's best to get a professional advisor when you begin to invest significant money, there is a lot you can and should do on your own, and I advise any woman who has never invested before to start with small amounts and *do it yourself.* As a woman, you have a natural intuition for what's right and just need to "feel" the investing world just as you would the stores and merchandise in a shopping mall.

There is a researched precedent for women's success in investing on their own. A national study found that women spend 40 percent more time than men researching before investing in a mutual fund, so the combination of instincts, patience, and homework pays off.[11] In additional, all-women investment clubs have an average annual return of 23.8 percent, whereas all-men clubs have returned only 19.2 percent.[12] Here are some tips:

1. *Start investing in mutual funds instead of individual stocks.* Mutual funds are like mix CDs, with lots of different recording artists on one CD. Mutual funds just have

multiple stocks instead of recording artists, but the principle is still the same: You're less likely to have a lot of stocks that don't perform if you are in a mutual fund, so you're less likely to have the whole batch go downhill. You can find the names of various mutual funds on MorningStar.com. The "safest" mutual funds are the exchange-traded funds: the Spiders (Standard & Poor's 500), Diamonds (500 Dow Jones Industrials), and the Cubes (NASDAQ) because these funds represent the entire stock index rather than one industry and so have more chance of success. You can invest online with a service such as ShareBuilder.com or BuyandHold.com. Either of these sites will walk you through the process of registering online and buying and selling mutual funds, and they will e-mail you updates.

2. *Invest with the future in mind, and never invest money that you cannot leave alone for 3 to 5 years.* There is the risk of loss with *any* investment that has a substantial upside, so an investment is not something you worry about daily. Accept that there will be ups and downs.

3. *If you do choose to invest in a specific stock rather than a mutual fund and aren't making a large investment, you can do it yourself on the Internet just like you did with mutual funds.*

4. *If your investment increases by 20 percent or more in 3 to 4 months, experts say to sell.* You've already made more than the averages, so don't get greedy and risk a loss. If you can't stand to sell all the stock and still believe that the company can grow more, then sell one-half.

5. *If you have a bad feeling about a company in which you own stock, get out.*

6. *If a stock drops 10 percent below your original investment, take note and consider selling.* If it drops 20 percent, get out while you can.

7. *Consider forming an investment club to keep you on track—and have fun.* You can do this by gathering a group of friends, pooling your financial resources, and deciding together what to buy and sell. You can learn more about how to do this at www.betterinvesting.org.

According to the National Association of Securities Dealers, one-half of all investors are women. This number is up an incredible 37 percent from 1990—it's certainly time for you to join in!

For more information on women and investing, take a look at womenswire.com/money, kaching.com, wife.org, and ivillagemoneylife.com.

I have enough money to last me the rest of my life, unless I buy something.

JACKIE MASON

15

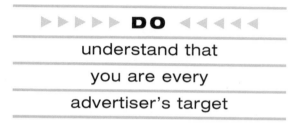

I have spent my career of 25 years in the field of advertising, and I know how powerful and important the messages sent to women are—even more powerful than the messages sent to men. Here's why.

Women are the key to almost every purchase and not just the obvious ones such as makeup and clothing. Women either purchase or are the dominant influence in the purchases of every household product and service—including health care, travel, appliances, and cars.

Advertisers and their ad agencies know this, so they design ads to capture our hearts (because we are heart people) and to make us feel that the product advertised will bring us a lot more than it actually can bring. Advertising planners call this a *key human value*, and it is the subject of a great deal of advertising research.

This is why toothpaste ads are designed to make you think that you'll find true love if you use a certain brand, and mattress ads are made to look like you will find true peace when you slumber on a mattress with that label.

In addition to a heavy dose of psychology, advertisers also spend an enormous amount of money—billions—to convince you that you aren't good enough without that new pair of jeans or that new credit card.

Don't believe them.

Your only revenge is to know your needs versus your wants, to understand your personal budget, and to stand firm in the midst of extreme media pressure.

Money and emotions are closely tied together, so women make a great target for unnecessary purchases. Thirty-six percent of women in a recent study said that they bought things impulsively they didn't need, whereas only 18 percent of men said the same.[13]

Something that many women find helpful is to ponder the following questions when faced with a nonessential purchasing decision:

1. What would I rather have in 5 years—this item or the same amount of money spent plus interest earned in a savings account?
2. How many of these do I already have at home?
3. Will buying this item bring me happiness?

It's also a great idea to give yourself what I call the *hour test*. If you *really* want to buy an item, take an hour away from the store, get a cup of coffee, and look at your checkbook register. After 1 hour, see if you still feel compelled to buy the item. On big-ticket items, I suggest waiting at least 24 hours before making the final decision to buy.

Chances are that after this pause, the thrill of the purchase has gone, and you can enjoy the thrill of shopping without the guilt of overspending.

Without a rich heart, wealth is an ugly beggar.

RALPH WALDO EMERSON

16

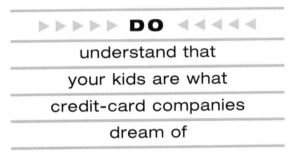
Want to know whom the credit-card companies really want to reach? Well, it's your kids—starting at about age 12 and going through college. Why would credit-card companies want to reach kids (teenagers, college students, and twenty-somethings) when they could focus exclusively on wage-earning adults?

Well, credit-card moguls know that kids are vulnerable, that kids are short on cash, and that kids are easy to snare into a lifetime of minimum-payment jail. Young people are great targets for credit-card companies because kids, accustomed to seeing their parents pay with plastic, are conditioned to believe that credit debt is a natural state. Also credit-card companies target college students because the students are relatively safe risks. In other words, the companies antici-pate that Mom or Dad will step in and pay the balances off if things get tight.

Also, cash-starved universities are making big-dollar deals with credit-card companies in the hopes that cards named for their schools will sentimentally stay in the hands of students as they enter the workforce. It's a great vehicle for the credit-card companies to establish a lifelong customer base and for the colleges to make extra money—but the students pay a high cost for this enterprise.

Unfortunately, the effects are sobering:

- The average college undergrad owes $2327 on credit cards.[14]
- Twenty-one percent of the undergraduates who have cards owe between $3000 and $7000.[15]
- Graduating students have an average of $20,402 in combined education loan and credit-card balances.[16]
- In March 2001, the U.S. Senate rejected 55 to 42 setting a $2500 limit on credit cards issued to people under age 21 unless a parent cosigned the account or the minor could demonstrate sufficient income.[17]
- Bankruptcies filed by people in their twenties are on the rise. In 1999, about 7 percent of personal bankruptcy filings were by minors.[18]

In other words, high school and college students are heavily in debt. What's worse, the epidemic is now creeping into junior high schools.

Many parents mistakenly believe that their children can't have a credit card without parental consent—but they are wrong. Even kids under age 18 can have cards. In fact, kids as young as 12 can get credit through cards issued in their name (but guaranteed by a parent) or prepaid, stored-value cards.[19]

Credit cards are an inevitable part of life, and certainly college students need to learn to manage credit responsibly.

But many parents are unaware that credit cards are so widely available on colleges campuses and that their kids easily can be heaping up debt without understanding the long-term consequences and without the knowledge of Mom or Dad.

The solution? Talk with your kids. Explain how credit cards work, and help them to manage their monthly bills. Talk about credit reports, and explain how their first credit card is an important part of developing a successful credit history.

Bottom line? Realize that you—the parent—need to teach financial literacy 101—it's not a course taught on campus.

Money is an article which may be used as a universal passport to everywhere except heaven, and as a universal provider for everything except happiness.

WALL STREET JOURNAL

17

▷ ▷ ▷ ▷ ▷ ▷ **DO** ◁ ◁ ◁ ◁ ◁ ◁

protect yourself
against identity theft

Just when we thought it was safe—ID theft looms as the next "must-worry."

Unfortunately, this is not media hype but rather a real problem, thanks, in part, to our digital society. ID theft is exactly what is sounds like: the theft of your personal identity by someone else. This means that the ID robber has somehow gained access to your Social Security Number, your credit cards, and your financial information—possibly even your personal bank accounts. As a result, the ID robber can pretend to be you and transact business in your name. This means spending the money in your bank account, charging on your charge cards, and making purchases online in your name.

The subject of ID theft is a book in itself, but here are a few pointers to help you understand how to protect yourself.

To minimize your risk for ID theft:

- Only give out your Social Security Number (SSN) when absolutely necessary. If you are asked in a routine way for your SSN, then ask if another type of ID can be used. Never give your SSN out to unsolicited callers or over the Internet.

- Don't carry your Social Security card with you.

- Keep items with personal information in a safe place, and never give out your SSN or your bank account numbers unless you are comfortable with the request.

- Tear or shred your charge receipts, credit-card applications, insurance forms, and bank checks and statements that you are discarding.

- Review your credit report from all three reporting agencies at least once a year. (See the Resources section in this book for this list.)

- Guard your mail from thieves. Pick up newly ordered checks from your bank, and do not have them mailed to you. If you are out of town, call the U.S. Postal Service at 1-800-275-8777 to request a vacation hold.

- Do not use easy-to-guess passwords. Purposefully misspelled words are a good choice because professional ID thieves actually have a system of determining passwords based on the most commonly used names and numbers. An easy password used for a simple online purchase makes it possible for an ID thief to get into your file and find your personal information.

- Stop receiving prescreened credit offers by calling 888-5-OPTOUT.

- Cover the screen with your hand when entering your automatic teller machine (ATM) password.

- If you become a victim of ID theft, immediately contact the three credit bureaus and have your creditors close all your accounts. Also request new bank account numbers and ATM and personal identification number (PIN) codes.

Contact 877-IDTHEFT, the federal hotline, and call your local police.

On average, consumers spend $1173 and countless hours to restore their credit ratings after ID theft, even though credit-card holders have to pay only the first $50 of the fraudulent charges on their accounts. ID theft costs the financial industry $2.4 billion yearly—so this is a serious matter.

Fortunately, ID theft is a relatively easy problem to avoid. It just takes vigilance and a little common sense.

The eye of prudence may never shut.

RALPH WALDO EMERSON

18

▶ ▶ ▶ ▶ ▶ **DO** ◀ ◀ ◀ ◀ ◀

keep track of

important documents

Ugh—paperwork.

But it is essential.

Throw it in a box, but keep the important documents or you will be sorry. The Internal Revenue Service (IRS) can look back for 3 years, but state taxing authorities can look back for many more years, so it's a good idea to keep records for more than 3 years. In addition, if there is any suspected fraud, the IRS can (and will) request documents for an unlimited period of time. Ultimately, it's your problem to provide the documents and the proof they substantiate.

What's important? Here's the *must keep* list:

- Your last 7 years of tax returns and accompanying records, such as credit-card receipts, investment statements, and business and other expenses
- Bank statements (ask the bank to store the original checks)
- The W-2 Form your employer gives you and any 1099 Forms you might receive for doing freelance work
- Documents for your big loans (car and home)
- 401(k) and other investment records

- Property tax records
- Year-end documentation that you receive showing interest paid or earned on all accounts
- Charitable contributions
- Income and expenses if you are self-employed (If you plan to deduct some of your housing expense for your business, then it is necessary to keep careful records of all household expenses such as utilities and also to determine the percentage of home space you are using for your business.)
- Estate returns and documentation for inherited items
- All insurance policies
- All legal agreements
- All credit-card paperwork
- Various certificates (birth, death, marriage, divorce, etc.)
- Passports
- Social Security records

It is critical for you to keep these records not only for IRS purposes but also for the inevitable error-correcting you will need to do when you find mistakes on your credit report. In all cases it's up to you to prove yourself right.

I don't like money, actually, but it quiets my nerves.

JOE LOUIS

19

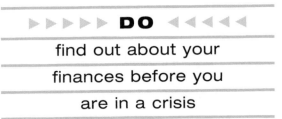

▶ ▶ ▶ ▶ ▶ **DO** ◀ ◀ ◀ ◀ ◀

find out about your

finances before you

are in a crisis

A prominent divorce attorney told me that he is constantly amazed at the number of sophisticated women who enter divorce proceedings with absolutely no understanding of their husband's financial assets or liabilities. In addition, many of these women have no idea what it takes to cover basic living expenses each month. The women he speaks of are well educated, bright, and resourceful but plead ignorance when it comes to all things financial.

He says it's a crime, and I agree.

Anyone in a marriage (which is, after all, a contractual agreement) needs to be aware at all times of the finances in the household. This doesn't mean asking if things are OK and then moving to the next topic.

It means understanding the money you have and the debts you have. This includes pension funds, credit cards, business deals, home finances, and insurance.

If you are not completely knowledgeable about your family's finances, you need to take these steps immediately:

1. *Tell your spouse you want to have a voice in the family's finances.* Obviously, your tone of voice in this request is

important, so be smart. Don't approach your request as a demand and put your spouse on the defensive. Approach the request as the loving, team-building action that it is.

2. *If your spouse is not agreeable to sharing financial information with you, then call his certified public accountant (CPA) and request a meeting.* If you are married, the CPA cannot withhold tax information from you—and tax information is a window to understanding all of the financial details in your family's life.

3. *Ask the CPA questions about your tax returns.* The CPA has a professional obligation to answer your questions truthfully and will be a great resource to you—provided that you don't call him or her to chat in March or April. (Also remember that CPAs are people too—try a lunch date for maximum input and help.) *No* question is a stupid question, so be blunt about what you do or don't understand. At the end of your session, ask the CPA if there are additional items he/she feels that you need to know about and yet have not questioned.

4. *Pay attention to every bank, investment, insurance, and retirement savings statement that comes to your home whether or not it is addressed to you, your spouse, or you as a couple.* If the statement is addressed to your spouse alone, ask your spouse questions to make sure you understand the account activities. Of course, assume that your spouse wants you to be aware of any items that might affect your family's financial future. If you sense that he is holding back information, then you may need to take the bolder step of calling the financial institution from which

the statements are issued and asking about the account or asking your CPA for additional information. *Watch for troubling signs: a husband who is secretive about financial matters, notices from collectors when you have no recollection of spending, or your spouse's unwillingness to take you on visits to the CPA or financial planner.* These can mean that he is in debt—and that means you could be in debt too.

5. *Always be prepared.* Keep 3 months of living expenses in a bank account with only your name, and keep 1 month of living expenses in cold, hard cash. How do you get these funds if you're not employed? Squeeze every gift dollar and every bit of your household allowance until you have this safety fund ready. If and when you need it, you'll be glad you did. Again assume that your spouse has your best interests at heart and wants you to have this protection—but if tensions arise, make sure you're protected no matter what.

Many women, even if they are the primary wage earners in a family, fear that questioning finances will dim the lights on love. However, loving yourself through vigilant self-care is a foundation you must build in order to truly love others.

There are people who have money and people who are rich.

Coco Chanel

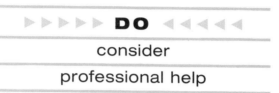

20

▷ ▷ ▷ ▷ ▷ **DO** ◁ ◁ ◁ ◁ ◁

consider

professional help

Today there are many self-help financial options on the Web, so it is possible to manage your financial life without the assistance of a personal financial planner. You can do it all on your own: tax returns, investments, retirement planning, debt planning, home mortgages, and insurance.

However, unless you have a great deal of time and want to become a subject expert, it's a good idea to at least review your self-managed finances with a professional every year or so. But proceed with caution. The field of financial consulting is growing so rapidly that it is difficult to know who does what. In addition, financial consultants charge for their services in many different ways—some hourly, some with a flat fee, and some with commissions—so it is important to understand how you will be charged before you set up a relationship.

Here's a helpful list of the various types of financial professionals, their payment methods, and services offered. If you are just starting out, you will probably want to work with someone who is fee-based and can give you an exact estimate for the scope of work you want completed *before* the work is begun. It is also wise to steer away from "free" advisors, who are compensated from the sale of products. Their motives may or may not be objective and your "free" advice may be very costly if you buy products that you do not need.

- *CPA.* A certified public accountant (CPA) does tax returns, auditing, and general accounting and can provide incidental advice. A CPA generally works on an hourly or project fee basis. CPAs are licensed and regulated by each state.

- *CFP.* A certified financial planner (CFP) gives financial counsel on a flat fee or commission basis. CFPs are not state regulated. Beware if your CFP works on a commission basis—it could indicate an incentive to sell you products you don't need.

- *Broker.* A broker is a person who buys and sells stocks, mutual funds, and/or insurance products. Brokers usually work on a commission basis. A broker generally has a Series 7 license, which allows him or her to buy and sell individual stocks. Some brokers also have Series 66 licenses, which allow them to buy and sell mutual funds and variable annuities.

- *Financial planner (or advisor).* Financial planners develop strategies for debt reduction, savings, retirement, college, and various life goals. They may work on a commission basis or for a flat fee, so check! Also, this title carries no credentials, so virtually anyone can set up shop as a financial planner—qualified or not. Check for education, experience, and client references.

- *Financial coach.* This is a new catch-all term for a broad category of advisors, including some debt consolidators. Just be sure to check the credentials because there is no formal certification for this title.
- *Credit counseling service.* This may be a for-profit or nonprofit entity specializing in credit repair and debt consolidation or counseling. To ensure that the service you are considering is a good one, check to see if it is a member of the National Foundation for Credit Counseling or the Association of Independent Consumer Credit Counseling Agencies. Both these groups establish standards that credit counseling firms must meet while providing services to consumers.

To help you with your search for credit counselors check these Web sites. In addition, ask your friends about the financial advisors with whom they have worked and *always* check references before you begin work with any financial advisor.

- *www.debtadvice.org.* The National Foundation for Credit Counseling
- *www.alccca.org.* The Association of Independent Consumer Credit Counseling Agencies
- *www.coanet.org.* The Council on Accreditation, the leading accrediting body for all credit counseling agencies

Money is better than poverty, if only for financial reasons.

WOODY ALLEN

21

DO

make small changes
that can save money

Not every financial decision has to be big. In fact, sometimes the small changes matter the most because they are the most realistic, and we actually can begin them immediately. Here are my top picks for changes that won't change your lifestyle—but will change your financial life:

- *Call your credit-card company and tell the representative that you are going to change cards in order to get a lower interest rate.* Keep talking until you get to a supervisor. You can then negotiate a better rate with your existing credit-card company because it doesn't want to lose your business. It is difficult but not impossible to do this. If your current card company won't budge, find another. Check out www.bankrate.com for the latest rate information.

- *Pay attention to bank charges on interest-bearing checking accounts.* Often the monthly fee is greater than the interest paid, so you are better off with a no-interest account. Look at your statements and examine your detailed charges so that you know what you are paying.

- *Look out for better long-distance and cellular phone rates.* These rates change constantly, so you have to be proactive to get the new discount. Most companies are glad to renegotiate a contract because it will tie you in to a longer arrangement, but who cares if you get a better deal? Call and ask for the latest promotion, but be careful. Free minutes are not what are important. The overall cost per minute counts most.

- *Buy generic.* Who really cares about brand names when it's a bottle under the kitchen sink? Ditto for expensively packaged body creams and bath products that are private labeled (in other words, packaged for a particular store as its own brand). The products inside the expensive private-label wrappings are generally made by the same manufacturers who provide products for lower-end retailers. The price different is generally not in the product quality but in the packaging.

- *Increase your 401(k) contributions by 1 percent.* (An extra $500 a year on a $50,000 salary could net you an extra $9565 in 10 years.)

- *Plan your major shopping excursions with cash.* Decide what you can afford to spend on back-to-school clothing (or whatever the need) and take that amount—no more and no less with you in cash when you shop. Leave your credit cards and checks at home. You can only spend what you have, and paying in cash will help you realize what you are paying. There is something about handing out hard-earned cash that makes you stop and think about the value of purchases.

- *Keep the professional manicures without the full costs.* Every other week have a full manicure and on the "off" weeks, ask for a polish change only. Your cuticles and your wallet will be happy.

- *Refinance your home mortgage.* But be careful. Sometimes a refinance does not save you money. To learn more about the mortgage financing process look at www.safe borrowing.com, which is operated by the American Bar Association.

- *Accessory pool.* Haven't we all carpooled? Well, with fashionable shoes, bags, and jewelry becoming the must-have accessories, and with prices for elegant accessories going sky-high, why not organize a group of women who share the same passion for style and create an accessory pool?

Money is the sixth sense which enables you to enjoy the other five.

W. Somerset Maugham

22

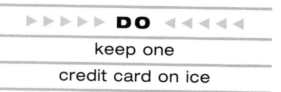

▶ ▶ ▶ ▶ ▶ **DO** ◀ ◀ ◀ ◀ ◀

keep one

credit card on ice

Sound crazy? Well, keeping a credit card on ice (literally) is one way of having your cake and eating it too.

It means just what it says. Take one active credit card, freeze it in a tray of water, and leave it there. When the urge strikes you to buy something of significance that you cannot otherwise afford, then go home and decide if it's worth thawing out the card to make the purchase.

This is not a miracle cure for spending, but it is a tried-and-true method of putting on the brakes so that you have to really consider your purchase.

Chances are that you will rarely use the card. But it will be there if and when you need it. Best of all, you will really have to consider the value of your purchase before using the credit card.

If you would be wealthy, think of saving as well as getting.

BENJAMIN FRANKLIN

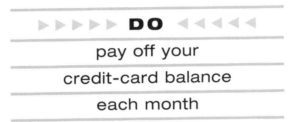

23

▷ ▷ ▷ ▷ ▷ **DO** ◁ ◁ ◁ ◁ ◁

pay off your
credit-card balance
each month

Do you need a credit card? Well, conventional wisdom is that you need one card and that the card should be in your personal name—not a joint account. However, don't have a credit card unless you can absolutely manage it carefully—and that means paying the balance off fully every month.

Many women mistakenly believe that it will be good for their credit histories if they keep a balance on a card, paying it off over time. But this is not true. All that is important is that you have a credit card and show that you can make timely payments. It is *not* important or wise to "carry" credit-card debt from month to month in order to show your creditworthiness.

So be careful.

Americans are drowning in credit-card debt, and you could, too. In 2000, the average cardholder had nine cards in his or her wallet, yet the credit-card companies still sent out an estimated 3.3 billion solicitations, averaging 30 per household. The average adult cardholder's outstanding balance today is $4400, whereas the average college student owes $2327 on credit cards.[20]

And the interest you *pay* on credit cards is always much higher than the interest you *make* on an investment account. This doesn't seem fair, does it? Well, it isn't. But you may be paying interest rates close to 20 percent and only making 5 percent. You do the math. It's an outrageous waste of money.

Instead, think about what paying interest on a credit card buys you: *nothing.* It buys the credit-card companies expensive commercials and fine offices—but it keeps you in financial prison.

You will never get ahead financially if you have credit-card debt. If you can't stop spending with a card in your pocket, then cut the card up, and mail it back to the credit-card company asking it to close your account. Make sure that it is noted on your credit report that the account is being closed at the customer's request. If you do not specify this information, it will be assumed on the credit report that you have been a credit risk, and, therefore, the card issuer has closed the account. This may seem like a small detail, but it has a major impact on your credit score.

Getting rid of your credit cards may be the only way to permanently end the temptation to overspend. But if you do choose to have a credit card, be sure to pay it off each month—and make sure that the payments are timely.

Honest poverty is a gem that even a king might be proud to call his own, but I wish to sell out.

MARK TWAIN

24

beware of
debt-consolidation plans

So you are up to your neck in credit-card debt, a home mortgage, and a car loan? It may seem very attractive to roll all these expenses into one easy monthly payment—a debt-consolidation plan—but use caution if you do this.

If you absolutely cannot pay your current bills any other way, then a debt-consolidation plan may be the only way to go because it will lower what you pay each month. But *never* use a debt-consolidation plan to free up more money so that you can accrue more debt. You see, the lower monthly payment that you get with a consolidation plan comes at a great cost—the cost of a higher interest rate and a longer payoff, both of which may cause you to pay much more on your loan long term than you would have before consolidation. If you must consolidate debts just to stay afloat, be very careful not to get into additional debt.

Also be cautious about including your home mortgage in a consolidation plan. This is a new trend and may offer some initially attractive rates, but if you add on 10 years of mortgage payments just to save a few hundred dollars each month, you are not winning financially. Consolidation that is based on home equity loans can be real trouble down the road because this causes you to replace exempt property (your homestead) with nonexempt property. If therefore you are in a state that allows homestead exemptions during bankruptcies, you are out of luck. In other words, if you consolidate debt and put your home mortgage in with other bills and then can't pay and have to file bankruptcy, your home may be taken as an asset to pay off debt. Then you're on the street with no assets.

If you still want to consider debt consolidation, be smart about your approach and understand all you can about your options. Visit a credit counseling agency or debt management company and look for a firm that is accredited by the Council on Accreditation (www.coanet.org).

To learn more about counseling agencies, check out www.debtadvice.org, www.alccca.org, and www.coanet.org.

By the way, the verdict is still out on whether help from a counseling agency will negatively affect your credit score (Beacon or FICO). The official word is that it will not; however, individual creditors sometimes will show concern if they see that you are in credit counseling. So use counseling if you are in trouble, but be aware that it may raise some eyebrows.

Again, the only long-term solution is to make more than you spend. If you merely consolidate what is already too much debt, you have not solved the problem. You have to spend less or earn more.

Money frees you from doing things you dis-like. Since I dislike doing nearly everything, money is handy.

GROUCHO MARX

25

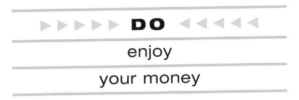

▶ ▶ ▶ ▶ ▶ **DO** ◀ ◀ ◀ ◀ ◀

enjoy

your money

If you follow every piece of advice in this book and manage your money meticulously but don't enjoy what you have—well, you may be missing the real point of this book.

Women often receive an early message that money is an enemy and not a friend. A recent study by the Women's Institute for Financial Education proves what I have found in my circle of friends—that only about 3 of 10 women have positive feelings about money.[21] Women also easily intertwine money and emotions, using money to unwisely provide emotional lifts. The psychological roots of our spending and attitudes toward money are so great that many of us still need major overhauls, but we are making progress.

The point of this book is not to go from one extreme to another. We don't need to turn into misers in order to be successful financially. And we do need to keep in mind that money really doesn't buy happiness, as evidenced by a fascinating study by happiness researcher Dr. David Myers. Dr. Myers has tracked the rise of income in America since the 1950s and has found that happiness has decreased while income has increased.[22] So we need to keep a healthy balance with our money, just as we do with other aspects of our lives, realizing that responsible financial management is just one facet of leading a healthy life.

Finally, remember that money is not an end. It is merely a means to each of our personal bests—the vision we have of living out rich and rewarding lives, whatever that vision may involve.

Money may not buy us love or happiness, but it does buy us opportunity. And that's all it takes for you to make the rest happen.

Life is not living, but living in health.

MARTIAL, *EPIGRAMS*

▼

Next,

25

DON'Ts

1

▶ ▶ ▶ ▶ **DON'T** ◀ ◀ ◀ ◀

think that everybody

knows more than you

I promise you that they don't.

I have watched woman after woman in financial sessions stare blankly as a financial consultant tried to express a particular concept or strategy. In every case the women were college educated and earned above-average incomes, yet they lived in a daze about financial management. As they sat in meetings with planners or consultants, they seemed afraid to ask questions, and the planners never seemed to pick up on the cues that the women were lost. Frequently, the women *acted* like they understood and went along with what they were told to do, regardless of the quality of the advice. But why?

It's as if women feel like we missed the day in school on which money was discussed and so are doomed to embarrassment for the rest of our lives. But it just isn't so. The fact is that we as women were never educated about money. We didn't miss the class. We were just sent into the world to sink or swim, and the sooner we realize that we're not alone, the better.

Experts agree that young boys and girls receive very different messages about money. Deborah Knuckey, author of *Conscious Spending for Couples,* writes that many parents emphasize the importance of money with boys but just don't teach their girls at all.[1] This finding is certainly consistent with my experience. As the parent of two teenage girls, I see a disturbing new trend: a generation of girls who envision themselves in careers but *don't* envision themselves handling money, which is a "chore" they consider boring.

So if you want to really change your financial future, make it your personal mantra to accept responsibility, learn everything you can, and take action.

You are not alone. You and I are in good company.

Knowledge is power.

FRANCIS BACON

2

▶ ▶ ▶ ▶ **DON'T** ◀ ◀ ◀ ◀

tell your friends

that you are on a budget

Remember—a budget is to money as a diet is to food. And what do all good friends say when you tell them that, once and for all, you're giving up Ben and Jerry's Karmel Sutra? Well, they say just one more scoop—and then you're off the wagon.

So it is with money. So budget, budget, budget. But never tell a soul. Or else you'll be off to the outlet store in no time, and all your good intentions will be out the window.

Instead, think Audrey Hepburn. You are demure, discreet—and just not in the mood for a shopping frenzy. Let them suspect that you have *better* things to do.

Use your budget as a means of finding your persona or expression—your own "cheap chic." Then, if you need to spill your guts, do so with a very select group of friends—the same group you'd trust with the other important issues in your life.

A good style should show no sign of effort.

SOMERSET MAUGHAM

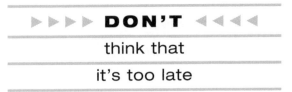

▶▶▶▶ DON'T ◀◀◀◀
think that
it's too late

Sure—it's better to learn all about money when you are in grade school and to start a savings account on your twelfth birthday, but it doesn't mean that it is hopeless if you started much later or not at all. So throw away all those books with examples of saving in college. And don't look back.

Whether you're 15 or 50, compound interest is compound interest. Whatever you save this week will reap dividends over time. And if you've made mistakes, don't dwell on them. Instead, put that energy into positive future efforts, such as taking care of your financial self.

Here's why.

Any amount of money you save will double approximately every 7 years—if you not only save the money but invest it somewhere at a rate of 10 percent. Naturally, if the money is invested at a lower rate, the money will grow more slowly, but 10 percent is an easy number to calculate for an example. If you save $5000 by age 30 *and never save another dime,* you'll have $10,000 at age 37, $20,000 at age 44, $40,000 at age 51, and $80,000 at age 58. This is the magic of compound interest, and it works for you at any age with any amount of money.

Here's an easy way to figure out exactly what you can make with the magic of compound interest—at various interest rates. It's called the *rule of 72,* and it quickly shows you how long it will take for your money to double.

First, be sure to know the interest rate you are getting on your money.

Then divide 72 by that interest rate. The answer will give you the number of years it will take for your money to double.

For example, if your interest rate is 4 percent, your money will double in 18 years. If your interest rate is 10 percent, your money will double in 7.2 years.

So start now—whatever your age and whatever you can afford—and you will see the results sooner than you think.

They always say that time changes things, but you actually have to change them yourself.

ANDY WARHOL

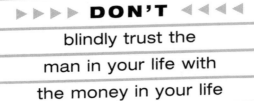

Speaking of better things to do—you have lots of options with your significant other besides trusting him with money. So enjoy those options but be ever so responsible with your own money. Suggest to him that you just don't want to bother his busy head with such trivia—then scurry off to check your money market.

Why such anti-Cinderella activity?

I don't wish a breakup on anyone, but the facts are that 43 percent of first marriages end in 15 years, and 39 percent of remarriages end within 10 years.[2] In addition, the standard of living for the lower wage earner plummets about 27 percent after divorce, whereas the higher wage earner's standard rises about 10 percent.[3]

Add to these statistics the fact that women live longer than men, earn less than men, and loose "earning time" by taking care of children and aging parents—and you have the reason that women need to make sure that they are financially stable within or without a marriage. We just can't count on a man to take care of us.

Here are the questions you need to ask yourself today:

- If my spouse divorced me today, could I survive financially on my own?
- If I lost my job today, would I have the available emergency funds to survive for 3 to 6 months without income?
- Am I listed in my spouse's will as his beneficiary, or is his first wife still listed because someone forgot to make the change? Are my children listed as beneficiaries in my first husband's will?
- Am I prepared financially for age 55, or am I expecting Social Security to sustain me?
- Do I have some major assets in my own name (such as a home or an investment account)?

The good news is that you *can* start investing and you are capable of doing it, so don't let the myths of women and money hold you back.

Riches are intended for the comfort of life, and not life for the purpose of hoarding riches.

SA'DI

5

▶ ▶ ▶ ▶ DON'T ◀ ◀ ◀ ◀

sign papers that
you don't understand

Read, read, read before you sign anything: an Internal Revenue Service (IRS) form, a home mortgage, a lease obligation, a credit-card application, or *any* legal document. If you don't *completely* understand and agree with what you are signing, then don't sign.

No one ever went to jail for being a few days late—even with IRS papers—yet, sadly, some women have served jail terms or paid significant sums of money for signing papers they did not understand.

Today the IRS is taking a kinder stance with women in these positions (called innocent spouse), but the bottom line is still the same, and it is very difficult to prove that you are an innocent spouse and therefore not responsible for what you have signed.

You are responsible for what you sign even if you don't read the fine print. Be it ever so boring, you have to read before you pick up the pen.

Why is this so important? In my talks with women I have heard countless stories about those who have inadvertently signed away their rights to contest a particular matter or who have given up the equity on their homes (perhaps for their spouses' business ventures). In all of these cases the women signed simply because their spouses said "it was fine," and they didn't realize the dire consequences until it was too late. Unfortunately, the law has no mercy for these women.

Your signature means that you are giving your consent, and it can be challenged only if you are able to prove without a shadow of a doubt that you were coerced into the signing, which is practically impossible to prove. So beware!

If you are unsure of something that your husband wants you to sign, try explaining your concerns in a nondefensive way. If you are in a volatile situation, it is worth going "overboard" in expressing your confidence in your husband's decisions so that he will feel comfortable talking to you. Otherwise, face it. Guys are easily threatened. If you come on too strong, he will likely shut down and resist talking honestly with you about the financial or legal matter at hand. So use your womanly skills.

On a lighter but still important note, it is critical to read every word of your credit-card agreements. You are most likely paying much more in fees and interest than you understand and will be shocked if you take the time to add up how much more you are spending on items bought years ago if you are only making minimum payments on your cards. Certainly this knowledge will make your more aware of new purchases and what these purchases will mean to your budget. In other words, is a new suit really worth a year of payments and 20 percent in interest charges? Probably not.

The important thing is to realize that you have power. No one can or should force you to ever sign anything about which you are not comfortable. If someone is trying to coerce you into signing a document, you can be assured that there is information that you need to know. You can also be assured that the person coercing you does not have your best interests at heart.

Take back your power.

Wealth is the means, and people are the ends. All our material riches will avail us little if we do not use them to expand the opportunities of our people.

JOHN F. KENNEDY

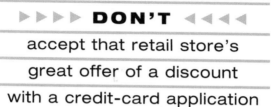

6

accept that retail store's

great offer of a discount

with a credit-card application

It may seem innocent, but it isn't.

Say you walk into the mall on Saturday afternoon and your favorite store is offering 20 percent off your same-day purchases if you open a credit-card account. Why not open an account, take advantage of the savings, and then tear up the credit card when it comes?

Because once you open a credit-card account, *even if* you never use it, it's on your credit report as open credit. This means that you *could* use it and get into debt, so the credit agencies downgrade you for this.

Once you have a card, you must cut it up and return it to the credit-card company with a letter asking the company to close the account per your request. Only then will it be closed on your credit report. It is also critical that you document that the account is being closed at your request and that this wording appears on your credit report. This is important because if the account is just shown as closed, other creditors will assume that you paid poorly and that the credit-card company closed the account because you were a poor risk. Not fair, but true.

Be sure to keep a copy of your letter closing the account in case the account shows up as open on a future credit report. Never assume that the account will "close itself" if you merely don't use it. Your credit report is composed of many things: how timely you pay, how much debt you have, how long you have had credit, the types of credit in use, and new credit. So every little piece of information is important in establishing good credit.

New credit shown on your credit report can mean the new car you just purchased or the account you just opened at the department store but never used. So, even if you don't use the store's card, it will lower your credit score because it is an opportunity for you to have debt. That's just the way the people who evaluate your creditworthiness will look at you.

Many people do not know about the intricacies of credit and don't realize that the credit cards they sign up for merely to get a discount can hurt when they apply for a car or other substantial loan because the lenders will assume that they are going to use the store's card, get into too much debt, and then not be able to pay all their bills.

Also be careful when you go car shopping. Of course, every car salesperson wants to make a deal and will ask for your Social Security Number so that he or she can tell you just what kind of deal is possible. If you are liberal about giving out your Social Security Number, you will find at the day's end that you have reduced your credit score substantially by having so many inquiries. My advice: Don't give out *any* personal information until you are ready to buy. Once a salesperson has your Social Security Number, he or she can inquire about your credit, and that in itself lowers your score—again, the inquiry is an indication to lenders that you are looking for more credit and so will get into too much debt.

The best thing is to limit your credit to one or two major cards and eliminate the individual store credit cards altogether.

Most of us aren't that interested in getting rich—we just don't want to get poor.

ANDY ROONEY

7

Have you noticed lots of pointers about credit reports in this book? Well, that's because your credit report is one of the most important documents affecting your financial life. And this "permanent" history of your financial life starts the minute you begin using credit or establishing debt such as a car loan.

It's a bit like Big Brother. There are three national companies (listed at the end of this chapter) that keep track of your financial dealings and record them in a document called a *credit report.* This report tracks your home mortgage, your car loans or leases, your credit cards, your bank accounts, any small financial mishaps (such as forgetting to return the video and then ignoring the store's mailings for penalty charges), and big financial issues like bankruptcy or judgments (which is when someone to whom you owe money documents a legal case against you).

The report grades you according to how much debt you have currently and have had in the past, how timely you make payments, the length of your credit history, and your new credit. The result of these five factors is summed up in what is called a *Beacon* or *FICO score*. A score of 620 or above is considered good, but there are many variables, so please read the Resources section of this book for more detailed information.

Traditionally, lenders viewed credit reports before assessing creditworthiness, but more recently, credit reports are being used for general character evaluation. In fact, many people can request a copy of your credit report. This includes potential employers, health insurers, car insurers, landlords, mortgage companies, car salespersons, and, of course, credit-card companies.

Today, credit reports are a source of information that employers will use to determine if they even want to hire you, landlords will use to determine if they want to lease to you, and health, car, and home insurance companies will use to determine rates on all types of insurance.

If the information on the report is incorrect (and it often is), it is *your* responsibility to correct it—and this process may take months. It is extremely unfair, but the only way you can prevent being judged unfairly is by regularly checking your own report and then taking action to correct errors. Frequent errors include a divorced spouse's debt still on your report, accounts closed incorrectly, and medical bills shown as unpaid when in fact they were paid by an insurance company.

It is important to check your credit report from each of the three reporting agencies because the information can be different on each version. It costs about $8 per report unless you have been denied credit, employment, housing, or insurance within the last 60 days. Then the report is free. The three credit-reporting agencies to check are:

Equifax
800-685-1111
www.equifax.com

Experian
888-397-3742
www.experian.com

TransUnion
800-888-4213
www.transunion.com

Check out www.ftc.gov to learn more about credit issues, or call 877-FTCHELP for additional printed information.

Any man can make mistakes but only an idiot persists in his error.

CICERO

8

▷▷▷▷ **DON'T** ◁◁◁◁
deny yourself
every material joy

Some financial books create unbelievable scenarios that require you to stop spending on just about everything (especially frappucinos and manicures) so that you can end up a millionaire 40 years later.

Well, they're right—but is that how you want to live? Most women I know don't. Remember, it's all about balance. And if you deny yourself everything, you're likely to go overboard someday and spend like crazy.

My idea of a good budget is like a good diet: It gives you just enough cake and wine to keep you motivated but not enough to ruin your looks. A good budget also keeps you from starvation-induced binges by allowing you a few treats here and there.

The point is that your budget has to work for you—not someone else. And it is all about choices and balance. So before you make a budget, think carefully about your lifestyle and what is important to you. Author David Bach, in his book, *Smart Women Finish Rich,* has a great exercise for visualizing dreams—and making the financial plans to achieve them.[4] His point is that your plan must be based on your unique dreams.

We all need motivation to keep going, and a starvation budget isn't going to motivate anyone. But dreams will.

So spend wisely but do make sure to include some of life's joys—whether they are small weekly splurges like a hair treatment, a seasonal pair of great stilettos, or a trip to the Riviera that requires saving for months or years. After all, if you can't enjoy life, what's the point?

A good budget will help you reach your dreams—not destroy them.

Make no little plans; they have no magic to stir men's blood.

DANIEL H. BURNHAM

▶ ▶ ▶ ▶ **DON'T** ◀ ◀ ◀ ◀

think that you have
to know everything

It's odd, but so many of us are more willing to admit hair color ignorance than financial ignorance. And why? I certainly took a full load of courses in college and never once had a class called "What You Must Know to Handle Money." So how was I supposed to know? No one assumed that I'd learn French without French lessons, but it was certainly assumed that I'd learn about money without financial lessons. It's like putting someone in a car and expecting them to drive safely the first time behind the wheel. And that's crazy.

The fact is that my experience is not isolated. Most of us were sent into the adult world totally unaware of the importance of properly handling basic financial matters, and unfortunately, financial literacy is still not a course provided in public schools. Then we wonder why college students get into debt.

The world of money is not fair. It is governed by rules that do not take into account the fact that we are multitasking to the max. It presents information in as complicated a manner as possible, and it offers no leeway when it comes to dead-lines. So it is entirely possible that your boyfriend can run over the cat, cheat on a résumé, forget your birthday, and yet have a great credit report, making his car loan interest rate very low, whereas you may be Miss Wonderful, but if you run to take dinner to a sick friend and forget about mailing those payments on time, you will suffer—even if they're only one day late.

This doesn't seem fair, does it? And it's not. As women we want to take care of others and assume that things will work out—that we will be repaid for our efforts. But it's time to wake up. Our financial lives are important because they enable us to take care of the other important things in our lives, such as loved ones, homes, and treasured belongings.

You really don't have to know everything—but you do need to know your personal basics (what you own, what you owe, and what you want), and you need to speak up when you have questions or concerns.

It is as simple as your physical health. If you are physically sick, it will limit your ability to enjoy life. If you are financially sick, it also will limit your ability to enjoy life.

Fortunately, there are no germs that cause financial illness—it's all a matter of your taking the time and interest to care for your financial life. And it is a matter of valuing yourself enough to know that it is not selfish to look after yourself financially. Consider financial fitness just as important as physical fitness and take the time to make sure you are in shape. Just as with an exercise program, the hardest part is starting.

But I do admit that the world of financial 'experts" don't make it easy for us. In fact, one possible obstacle to progress is the stereotype (somewhat deserved, in my opinion) that brokers treat women as stupid. In fact, a recent Oppenheimer Funds study points out that only 27 percent of men and 31 percent of women believe that women receive equal treatment from stockbrokers and financial planners.[5]

You don't have to know everything, but you do need to recognize what you don't know. And then you must be confident enough to ask questions until you are satisfied.

There really is no stupid question.

The great aim of education is not knowledge but action.

HERBERT SPENCER

10

▶ ▶ ▶ ▶ **DON'T** ◀ ◀ ◀ ◀

think poor

What is thinking poor?

It's a state of mind that is extremely dangerous—an approach to life that keeps you imprisoned. If you are thinking poor, you don't really believe that you can get out of debt or that financial success is achievable.

You just don't believe that you deserve it.

As a consequence, you stay in debt. You may spend unnecessarily to make yourself feel better, or you may have a "devil may care" attitude when you are out with your friends, but inwardly, you feel miserable. Thinking poor is a self-fulfilling prophecy that robs you of the freedom that financial security can bring.

So if you are in the dumps and thinking poor, the first thing you need to do is change your thinking.

If you are broke, recognize that you are not poor. There is a major distinction between being broke and being poor. Being broke is merely a temporary situation that can be remedied. But being poor is a mind-set that you must change in order to be financially successful.

In order to switch mind-sets, you'll need to restart your financial life self-image by envisioning where you want to be—what is the life you want to lead? Literally close your eyes and imagine the life you want. Is it a simple life out of the fast lane with few responsibilities? Is it a fast-track career path with heavy stress but optimal financial rewards? Only you know what's in your heart.

Listen to yourself, and write down a description of the life you want. Be bold.

Next, trace your steps backward from the life you have envisioned to where you are currently. Imagine that getting from where you are to where you want to be is a board game. Make a written list of three things you can do to move ahead. Then, every month, reevaluate and make a new written list of three things.

Sound simple? It is—and anything more complicated probably won't work.

The first step in making any financial change requires acknowledgment of the need to change and a conscious decision to act differently. The conscious decision you could make at this very moment is to stop thinking poor.

Replace the poor thinking with a vision of where you want to be. Write the vision down and say it out loud every day.

Rescue your dreams.

ANONYMOUS

11

▶ ▶ ▶ ▶ **DON'T** ◀ ◀ ◀ ◀

blindly trust your
financial advisor

Financial advisors these days come in all shapes and sizes. But one thing is true regardless: Only trust what they say if you completely understand what they are saying and if you know how every decision will affect you.

It's not that these advisors aren't looking out for your best interests; they want to help, but advisors don't always understand each particular situation. And advisors are not *always* right. Financial advisors assume that if we want to buy a house well above our means, we know what we're doing. We, on the other hand, assume that our advisors will tell us if we are doing something dumb.

I know that financial advisors are not always right because I have personally experienced the pain of bad advice. I once paid a financial consultant to help me invest in a house that was in an affluent area—a sure bet financially, he said. When I finally realized that the mortgage payments were too much of a stretch for me, I sold the house 3 years later, and lost $350,000. On top of that surprise loss, I found out that the investment (unlike business losses) was not tax deductible, which was another shock to me. My only gain was knowledge and an increased sense that I had to be more in control of my own financial life.

No one cares as much about your future as you do—so shore up your confidence, steel yourself, and, if you are using an advisor, ask this get-to-the-bottom question: "Is there anything about this decision you'd want me know if I was your [choose one: sister, mother, girlfriend]?" Then listen.

It's just not OK to be uninformed. Yet many women with incredible educations and high-powered jobs still avoid tackling the real issues of money management. According to Patricia Ireland, a financial consultant at Salomon Smith Barney, who leads financial planning seminars for a New York alumnae group called Columbia College Women, many Ivy League women have no clue how to begin securing a financial future for themselves.[6]

My point? You are not alone, and the financial industry knows it—yet the professionals are still largely unprepared to deal with women's issues.

The onus is on you to make sure that your money is managed properly and that you have the proper types of insurance, investments, and retirement plan. You need to be involved in the big picture plans as well as the details. For example, you need to know exactly where your money is invested and what type of return the money is earning. You need to know the details of all your insurance policies. You need to know your credit scores and what you owe on each credit account.

When you receive mailings or Internet statements, you must check the activity section of your monthly statements regarding any investments you have. (Increasingly, investment firms are taking the stance that any mistake not caught within 30 days is no longer their responsibility. This means that $1000 entered inaccurately instead of $100 could be your problem—even if it was the investment firm's error.)

By the way, financial advisors generally fall into two categories: fee-based and commission-based. If you are just beginning, you probably will be more comfortable with a fee-based advisor. Then you will know what the advice is costing you and you will be assured that the advisor has no ulterior motive to sell you unnecessary products. Of course, always ask for an estimate and term sheet before you agree to any consulting relationship.

For more information on financial advisors, take a look at these Web sites: www.fpanet.com and www.nafpa.com.

You'll be ahead of the game if you do your homework before speaking personally with anyone.

To learn the value of money, it is not necessary to know the nice things it can get for you, you have to have experienced the trouble of getting it.

PHILIPPE HÉRIAT

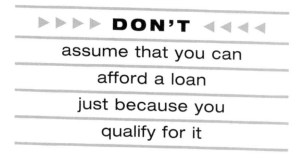

12

▶ ▶ ▶ ▶ **DON'T** ◀ ◀ ◀ ◀

assume that you can

afford a loan

just because you

qualify for it

Doesn't it feel great to hear, "You're approved"? (Guess that's why Barbie Cash Register comes with a full-sized American Express card and a machine that rings bells when she is approved—honestly.)

The only problem is that "You're approved" may mean that you are in over your head. And this could be true for a home mortgage, a car loan, a furniture purchase, or credit cards. Remember that the company providing the loan makes more money the longer you take to pay for the purchase. In addition, the loan provider may make a substantial amount in penalty fees if you are late. So it is in the loan provider's best interest—not yours—to make sure that your credit is approved.

The most common example of this is the innocent call a retailer will make to allow you, "a good customer," to extend your credit limit for that extra piece of clothing you want to purchase. What the retailer fails to say is that the credit limit increase will post negatively on your credit report and possibly change your interest rate.

A less common but far more destructive example is with home mortgages, where well-intentioned people take on way more debt than they can handle. As a result, the largest percentage of home foreclosures occurs in the first 6 months after a home purchase. Again, I experienced this saga (without a foreclosure) when I purchased a home well above my means—even though I "qualified" for the loan.

A recent Harvard study shows that the number of homeowners who can't make their payments and are foreclosing has almost doubled in the last 2 years despite the low interest rates. What's happening? Low interest is enticing people into buying homes that really stretch them beyond their limits. In 2002, almost $100 billion in cashout refinancings were completed compared to only $20 billion in 1993.[7]

Finally, many debt-consolidation programs are really only ways to free up more credit and may cause disastrous results.

The bottom line is that you must be responsible for understanding what you can afford—and this means afford *with* paying all debts on time and credit cards in full each month. This is not the advice that lenders will give you (how would they stay in business?), but it is the advice you need to give yourself.

What if you are not sure if you can afford something? Well, that little doubt is a great indication that you really

can't afford what you are about to do. Remember, there will always be things to buy and debt to get into. If your stomach aches one bit at the thought of a loan, just say no.

Nothing can bring you peace but yourself.

RALPH WALDO EMERSON

13

> ▶ ▶ ▶ ▶ **DON'T** ◀ ◀ ◀ ◀

make minimum payments
on your credit cards

OK—here it may seem that I am contradicting what I said earlier about making payments on time. So let me clarify. It is better to make a *small* payment early than a *big* payment late. If the choice is between food and a larger payment, you obviously need the food. Make a minimum payment on time if that's all you can do. But please keep in mind how much more expensive that minimum payment is than it looks.

For example, if you have a balance of $2500 on a credit card and only make minimum payments of $10 per month, it will take approximately 14 years and 11 months to pay the $2500, and the total you will pay will be an astonishing $2224 in interest in addition to the $2500. (This will vary from credit card to credit card, but it is the average.) This is compound interest in reverse—and it is the way many of us get and remain in financial jail.

The solution? Think before you buy. If the purchase requires long-term payments, is it worth five times the original price? (This is approximately what the real cost will be.) Will you really care about those clothes 5 years from now? You also can look at the investment opportunity you are missing by not saving even $10 per month—it adds up to real money.

So it's really your choice: Fill your own pockets, or fill the pockets of the big financial institutions.

Imagine this: what would happen if every person paid their credit cards in full every month and never carried a balance forward? Well, the credit-card companies would go out of business, but we, the consumers, would have a great deal more in savings and would sleep much better each night.

Happiness is in the taste, and not in the things.

FRANÇOIS LA ROCHEFOUCAULD

14

Yes, if you're a parent, you want the best for your children. But the best does not necessarily mean total insulation from financial realities. In fact, learning to live within a tight budget, cope with setbacks, and work hard are important lessons to observe—and learn—at a young age.

Experts agree that kids pay a high price for a silver-spoon life and that children of the very wealthy are at risk for self-doubt, identity conflicts, and risky behavior. In fact, so many families are passing on so much money today that a boutique industry has been spawned to advise trust officers in financial institutions on alcohol and drug abuse.

So stop thinking that money cures all evils, and start counting your blessings if you are not megawealthy.

Wealthy, broke, or in-between, it is critical to capture every opportunity to teach your children about money. And "down" times provide the best opportunities. Just as you would never put your child behind the wheel of a car and say "drive" without first teaching your child *how* to drive, you should never put your child into situations where his or her financial well-being is at risk without first teaching the basics and taking your child for a test drive or two.

Kids know what's going on whether you tell them or not, so, if things are tight, don't add pressure by keeping financial concerns a big worry. Just as with other family issues, kids can tell if something is not right, and the story they will concoct in their imaginations is likely to be much worse than the reality of your situation. Instead of hiding financial realities (positive or negative) from your kids, explain your situation in age-appropriate ways (remember, it's like sex—not every kid wants or needs to know everything at once). And model the financial behavior you want your kids to emulate—positive, thoughtful, and persevering.

As a mom of teenage girls, I can vouch for the fact that kids appreciate the opportunity to be a part of the solution—whether it's cutting back on a clothing budget, earning income for personal extras, or contributing to household chores. It's all in the team spirit you develop—or don't.

The easiest way for your children to learn about money is for you not to have any.

KATHARINE WHITEHORN

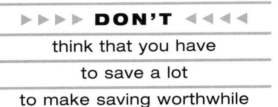

15

▶ ▶ ▶ ▶ **DON'T** ◀ ◀ ◀ ◀

think that you have

to save a lot

to make saving worthwhile

Oh, the magic of compound interest. It's like squeezing all the bad out of credit-card debt and turning it into your personal money machine. And it doesn't take a lot of money to start—in fact, it takes very little. Yet many women fail to ever start investing because they think that it will require them to have thousands of extra dollars. Or, worse yet, women think it's too late. Both of these are perceptions you must overcome in order to be successful financially.

Here are some examples that show the power of saving and investing very small amounts. Let's start with $25 per month—an amount *anyone* could handle, and many online investment opportunities have a $25 minimum.

If you saved and invested $25 per month for 5 years and received 5 percent interest each year, you'd make more than you imagine. After 5 years, you would have put away $600 but actually have $712. Now, what if you left that money *alone* for 48 more years? You'd have a total of $9302. This is the magic of compound interest. Your money keeps growing even if you do nothing.

In fact, it only takes investing $15 per month for 50 years at an interest rate of 10 percent to accumulate $250,000.

The point is that *time is really more important than the amount you save,* so *start now*—and that means at *whatever age you are now.* Saving and investing are habits, so starting today with a tiny amount is very important—more important than waiting for that big raise to provide you with a windfall.

Find *some* money and invest it. If you want to make sure that you keep on track, find four friends and have a monthly investment club.

Whatever it takes—just start.

Tomorrow is the most important thing in life. Comes into us at midnight very clean. It's perfect when it arrives and it puts itself in our hands. It hopes that we've learned something from yesterday.

JOHN WAYNE

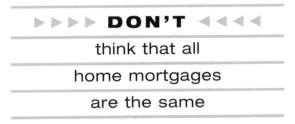

16

▶ ▶ ▶ ▶ **DON'T** ◀ ◀ ◀ ◀

think that all

home mortgages

are the same

Quick—Do you own a home? Do you know the interest rate on your mortgage? Is your rate fixed or adjustable? Do you have a prepayment penalty? What is the amount of equity you have in your home? What is your monthly payment and does it include taxes and insurance, or are those extra? Do you know if your mortgage is the best one you can get?

If you are like most women, you aren't really sure of the answers to these questions—and you probably assume that any of the big-name mortgage companies charge about the same for their services.

Well, you are wrong. Like most of life, home mortgages are highly negotiable—but again, it's up to you to push for the best rate. Shopping around can save you enormous amounts of money over the long run, so even though it may be time-consuming, shopping mortgages is financially beneficial. Here are some pointers for your shopping:

- *When you call a company for rate information, don't set-tle for the first answer or the first person who picks up the phone.* (A friend in the private mortgage business equates this with getting your hair cut by whomever picks up the phone in a salon.) Always ask the position of the person with whom you are speaking and keep asking for higher levels until you reach a manager.

- *Beware: All the people who work with you to provide home mortgages work on commissions and have the latitude to add a point or so (this means 1 percent of the loan amount) to any loan.* Of course, the extra point means more money for the person handling the mortgage and less money for you to keep. One percent may not seem like much, but on a home loan it can be substantial.

- *Make sure that your loan does not have a prepayment penalty.* A prepayment penalty would make it impossible for you to pay your mortgage quicker than required—without being charged extra interest. Many mortgage companies automatically include this in their loans—but are quite happy to delete the prepayment penalty *if* you are wise enough to notice it and ask.

- *Understand that a quoted rate does not equal the rate you will get.* It's not your interest rate until it's locked in. So if you spend weeks getting quotes and then go back to your first choice, you may have a surprise. Always ask if the rate is locked in.

- *Shop around—and ask for better rates and fewer points.* Remember, your mortgage broker does have the latitude to give you a better deal—but only if you push. Treat the broker like any business arrangement (or car purchase), and assume that the first rate quoted has room for negotiation. Tell the broker that you are shopping with other companies, and let him or her know that you are knowledgeable and not afraid to walk away from the offer. The most important thing is to not appear desperate. Your greatest power comes when you are not afraid to say no.

- *Do some calculations yourself so that you can talk intelligently with the mortgage brokers.* Try these Web sites to see what a difference a rate can make: www.mortgage-calc.com and www.mortgagenet.com.

Finance is the art of passing money from hand to hand until it finally disappears.

ROBERT W. SARNOFF

17

▶▶▶▶ DON'T ◀◀◀◀

be clueless about
your expenses

Nine of ten women I've counseled regarding money have absolutely no idea what it takes to live their lifestyle each month. Is it because women are incapable? No, it's because we are frazzled, overbooked, and just don't have one more ounce of energy to figure anything else out.

So don't beat yourself up. But do commit to paper what your expenses really are so that you can plan.

I am not one to advocate writing down the cost of every coffee over a lifetime. However, if you really want to know what you need to live (and you should), write down your expenses for 1 month.

An easy way to do this is to start the month with several envelopes filled with cash for each of your big "fritter away" items: beauty, gifts, eating out. As you go through the month, simply spend cash from the appropriate envelope. This avoids the hassle of writing everything down. At the end of the month you'll be able to see where you are: what category envelopes still have money and what envelopes are empty (or negative). Since these "fritter" areas are where we all tend to spend more than we think we do, these are the areas to really study. It's also a lot more motivating to have spending money than it is to think about budgeting, yet the bottom line is the same: This envelope exercise will help you to understand what you may unknowingly be spending each month. Of course, you also need to be aware of your big fixed expenses like your car and home costs, but I am presuming that you know these.

Do the envelope exercise for 1 month and most likely you will be amazed—most women find that their actual living expenses are 25 percent more than they have budgeted—and then we wonder why we have so little left?

But don't make this an exercise in guilt—*any* budget is fine as long as you are honest about it and can afford it.

Every woman should be able to take care of herself, and the first step is knowledge. Ask questions, take notes, meet with your certified public accountant (CPA), and read and share your knowledge with other women.

Most of all, know what it takes for you to live the life you want. Be honest with yourself. And make sure that you develop the independent financial resources to make that life happen.

A billion here, a billion there, pretty soon it adds up to real money.

SENATOR EVERETT DIRKSEN

18

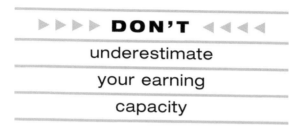

A friend of mine with a high-end job in New York City recently confided to me that she was always shocked when she received a raise. Another girlfriend in a small town took a job for $10,000 a year less than what she knew she was worth—just to not "rock the boat" at the beginning of a new job.

Both women were victims of their affluent upbringings and their desire to make sure that they were well liked. And many of us are in this same "good girl" category.

I was taught to believe that "good girls" don't make a fuss over money and that part of my life success would depend on my ability to act a little less "worthy" than I really was. Boy, was that advice bad. It kept me from asking the tough questions about my compensation and about the compensation of others in my professional peer group. In other words, that thinking kept me down.

The point? Never, ever be ashamed to ask about what other professionals in your field are making. Never be ashamed to ask questions about how money is being spent in your business environment. Never forget to value yourself.

Here are some on-the-job tips to make sure that you are compensated according to your worth:

- *Get your compensation agreement in writing.* Verbal agreements are fruitless if there is ever a conflict. Always ask your supervisor to document agreements about time, money, or benefits. If he or she does not comply, simply send a follow-up e-mail or letter to your supervisor after any compensation discussion.

- *Negotiate your benefits.* Everything is negotiable, and time or extra benefits may be more valuable than money at certain points in your life. If your spouse has good health insurance, you may want to drop this benefit in exchange for time off or additional compensation. Also consider the extra costs of your employment, such as your cell phone and laptop, and make sure that you are appropriately compensated for their use or that you are utilizing these expenses to your income tax advantage.

- *Turn in your expense reports in a timely fashion.* Hint: it's a real executive turnoff if you turn in your expense report late and then ask for your reimbursement check to be expedited. As an employer, I was always amazed at how long it took for my staff to turn in sizeable expense reports. Yet cash flow has real bottom line implications. So don't wait for your credit-card bill to be due before you write up your expense report. The extra 30 days can make a difference in the interest you can make in your accounts.

- *Always know your boss's boss.* Make sure that he or she knows about the great job you are doing so that when it is time for a salary review, you are sure that the ultimate decision maker (or close to it) knows how great you are. Never assume that your boss is telling his or her boss how great you are doing—make it a point to communicate this yourself.

- *Ask for performance reviews.* These keep you in sync with your boss—and also keep you on top of future salary negotiations. In many organizations, especially entrepreneurial ones, salary negotiations are not handled on a formal basis; instead, they are subject to the whim of someone noticing how great a job you are doing. Make sure that they are always aware that you are an asset and make a difference to the company's bottom line.

- *Keep your options open.* If you are contacted by a headhunter, take the opportunity to talk and explore your value in the workforce—even if you are not looking for a new job. Just because you are "not looking" doesn't mean you shouldn't stay informed.

- *Don't be afraid to earn more than your husband.* Although the average woman's wage is still less than a man's (78 cents to the dollar), scores of women are breaking into higher-paying professions, resulting in the fact that in 30.7 percent of households of married couples with a working wife in 2001, the wife's earnings outweighed the husband's.[8]

- *Be bold about seeking venture capital (a business loan) for a new business idea.* Although women create 70 percent of jobs at privately run companies and own 26 percent of all companies, women receive only 4.4 percent of all venture capital funds.[9] The message? There is investment money for our ideas, but we need to pursue it.

Know what you are worth. It's the first step toward getting it.

Work is our sanity, our self-respect, our salvation. So far from being a curse, work is the greatest blessing.

HENRY FORD

19

We may think that our credit cards have lives of their own, but of course, we are the ones responsible for spending and saving—and living with the results. So, if something is wrong, the first step in changing it is to face the facts and make the necessary lifestyle adjustments. Bottom line: Be honest, and lower your spending. There is no other cure. And facing the truth is the first step you *must* take to gain financial health.

If you want to know how you are doing financially, do a quick gut check—and trust what you are feeling. Do you get stressed out each month at bill-paying time? This alone is a sign that you are in trouble. Does your stomach ache each time your debit card hits the ATM in search of money? Your are in real trouble. However, if you want a more specific method, try this: Write down your monthly income, before taxes. Then write down your monthly loan expenses, including home, cars, and credit cards. If your debt is more than 40 percent of your income, you are headed for trouble. If it is 50 percent, you are in real trouble. Get moving to change things now.

Here are the five musts that financial experts agree are needed to get out of financial trouble or to stay out of harm's way:

1. Do a written inventory of your financial life noting everything that you owe, everything that you own, and what you spend on a weekly basis. Be brutally honest. Don't try to pretend that you will have that department store debt paid next month—this thinking is as likely to fail as buying a pair of jeans one size too small in hopes that you'll fit into them by the time you need to wear them.

2. Lower your everyday spending in every way that you can by cutting out the extras, such as fast food, unused health club memberships, and grocery store last-minute items like magazines that you'll never have time to read.

3. Pay off high-interest-rate credit cards as soon as possible. In the interim, negotiate lower interest rates on the cards by patiently talking with manager after manager and threatening to change cards.

4. Put as much in retirement savings as you can. The maximum 2003 allowance is $12,000 for company 401(k) plans. Remember that this money is not subject to income tax.

5. Establish an emergency fund so that you can live a minimum of 3 months without income if necessary.

According to the Federal Reserve, consumers today are weighed down with debt of $7.3 trillion. And this is twice the amount of consumer debt we carried a decade ago.

If you are in over your head, you are certainly not alone—but in this case, it's bad company to keep.

Take the five action steps listed above to reclaim your financial health.

It is hard to pay for bread that has been eaten.

DANISH PROVERB

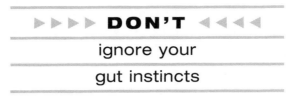

20

►►►► DON'T ◄◄◄◄

ignore your
gut instincts

I believe that we all have a sense of intuition for a reason—and I bet that you regret every time you haven't followed your intuition about a child's minor fever or even a diet fad. Why, then, do we, the gender with the stronger intuition, not follow our financial instincts?

Perhaps we ignore our good instincts because we always think that someone else knows more about money than we do—a spouse, a financial advisor, or an employer. We also tend to think that we need to take care of everyone else before we take care of ourselves. But here's another secret:

In my interviews for this book, I encountered woman after woman who reported feeling unsettled after accepting a piece of advice—and later regretting that she did not listen to that little voice inside. One woman in particular bought a great deal of stock "on margin" (meaning she borrowed to buy the stock) and now is saddled with a large amount of debt—all because she allowed her broker to sweep her into the exhilaration of the last stock upswing and didn't listen to her own instincts.

So, yes, gather information. Read. Learn. Financial advisors are great sources of information and insight. But take time to listen to your own sense of right and wrong when it comes to the final decisions about money that may permanently affect your life.

It's a known fact that women are more successful stock market investors than men. Researchers believe that this is due to our natural ability to pick up on what's going to work. In other words, when we walk into a store, we can generally tell if the mix of merchandise and the environment are going to succeed. It just "feels" right to us. This same sense of what will and won't be successful gives us an advantage in the financial world—we only have to use it.

Silver and gold are not the only coin; virtue too passes current all over the world.

EURIPIDES

21

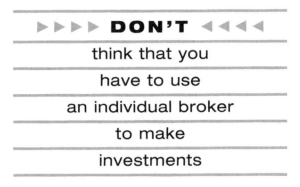

▶ ▶ ▶ ▶ **DON'T** ◀ ◀ ◀ ◀

think that you

have to use

an individual broker

to make

investments

Sure—if you have tens of thousands of dollars to invest, a real-life broker can be very helpful. However, if you are starting out, at any age, you can and should make small investments on your own. Not only does self-investing save money—it also gives you a chance to learn from the inside out so that you will become more knowledgeable in the future if and when you decide to use the services of a broker.

The secret is in just trying—and it's much easier than programming your media system.

The key is that you don't have to start with a lot of money. In most cases, online services have a $25 minimum. Technically speaking, online services *are* like brokers. They are just not individuals in the sense of personal, walking and talking financial advisors.

My favorite Internet sites for investing in the stock market are sharebuilder.com and buyandhold.com. You can buy individual stocks or invest in an index (a well-known mix of stocks) with these sites, and they really walk you through the how-to's.

Start by investing in a company you know and for which you have a good gut instinct. Consider the products you buy and the stores in which you frequently shop. These are most likely good investments, and you will feel comfortable with them. After you invest, step back and leave the investment alone. Avoid the temptation to react to short-term changes. Stock investments are not suited for short-term gain, so don't look at your investment every day. Just keep the money there and watch it grow over time. In fact, a recent study by the University of California found that men trade stocks more frequently than women—and have lower returns to show for their lack of patience.[10]

So a hands-off strategy really is best.

If you want to invest but are interested in something other than the stock market, you might want to consider bonds. Savings bonds are very safe investments. What are savings bonds? Bonds are like IOUs issued from a business or government. They are really just like the IOU's you gave to your parents as a kid, only safer. Generally, they pay interest in two annual installments.

Treasury bonds are 100 percent safe and may be purchased free of local taxes and without commissions or fees at www.publicdebt.treas.gov. To learn more about bonds in general, try www.savingsbonds.gov.

Bonds may not be as sexy as stocks, but they are a safe way to start investing and have made a big comeback in the last 2 years.

Stocks or bonds, investments are easy to make once you take the first step.

Wealth unused might as well not exist.

AESOP'S FABLES

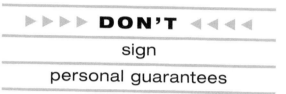

22

If you are a business owner (and more of us are every day), then you may be operating as a sole proprietor, a partnership, or a corporation. If you are operating as a corporation, you have automatic protection from creditors should your business fail. The downside of that protection is that you may be asked to sign a personal guarantee, which means just what it says: You are promising to pay personally something the business owes. But even if you are not operating under the protection of a corporation, you may be asked to sign a personal guarantee.

Often, this guarantee is requested on office and equipment leases. But beware—once you sign, you are responsible for every penny of the lease for every year of the lease (which could be hundreds of thousands of dollars)—even if you close up shop and turn in the keys years in advance of your completed lease. Generally, in the case of office space, it does not even matter if the landlord leases the space again the day after you move out. You are still on the line for all the years agreed to in your lease.

So it's best to never sign a personal guarantee. You can most likely find another office or other equipment to lease. Remember, the leasors need you more than you need them.

If you are in a situation that absolutely demands your personal guarantee, then give it with a great deal of caution and negotiate well. Be sure that your lawyer oversees what you sign and that you don't sign away too much; in other words, on a lease obligation, you might negotiate to guarantee a certain period of time and yet not guarantee the entire life of the lease. Or you might guarantee under certain circumstances and specify circumstances in which you would not guarantee, providing you with an "out."

Make doubly sure that you do not guarantee someone else's obligations, which can happen more easily than you might imagine. Depending on the state in which you live, you may have an implicit obligation to any guarantee your spouse signs—unless your obligation is specifically written *out* of the agreement. So it is critical that you have an understanding of your spouse's obligations as well as your own.

Make sure that you know what you are obligated for—and don't stop negotiating until you are certain that the deal is right for you.

When you get into a tight place and everything goes against you, till it seems as though you could not hang on for a minute longer, never give up then, for that is just the place and time that the tide will turn.

HARRIET BEECHER STOWE

23

Oh, I wish I had a dollar for every female friend who was waiting for Prince Charming to save her from financial disaster. But it's just not going to happen. You can buy a lottery ticket, date the right guy, and consult your horoscope, but the fact is that *you*—and you alone—are in charge of your financial life.

If you don't agree, take a look at these sobering statistics:

- Fifty-nine percent of working-age women are clueless about how much money they need to save for retirement.[11]

- A woman's standard of living can plummet 10 to 25 percent after divorce.[12]

- One year after divorce, the average woman is single and has an income of $11,300.[13]

- Half of all women today work in traditionally female, low-paying jobs without pensions.[14]

Why is this so? Financial experts agree that women still have not broken the financial ceiling and that far too often women (even women who have broken the glass ceiling) are leaving money management issues to the men in their lives—or just ignoring these issues completely.

In general, women are ignorant of their spouses' finances and complacent about their own. As a result, there are enormous numbers of capable women who are not achieving their financial potentials.

What is the answer?

Well, first, let these statistics be your wake-up call. No one is immune from financial difficulties. Then take action to really examine your life and make sure that you have knowledge and control over your personal finances. Stop acting like everything is OK if it isn't. Be real with yourself, and follow the tips in this book to remedy specific areas of difficulty.

Finally, never, ever leave your financial health to someone else—even if he does look like Prince Charming.

America has the best-dressed poverty the world has ever known.

MICHAEL HARRINGTON

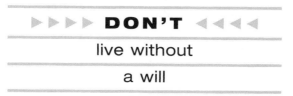

24

live without
a will

Of course, no one wants to think about dying. But not think-ing about dying will cause your loved ones an immense amount of unnecessary grief. Currently, two out of three Americans die without a will.[15] This means that the fate of what they leave behind—money, homes, children—will be in the hands of Uncle Sam, the court system, and disputing rel-atives. In other words, it will be a mess and their wishes will most likely not be carried out.

There is just no excuse for living without a will or a liv-ing trust. A *will* is a document that specifies what happens to your assets after your death, and a *living trust* is a document that sets up management of your assets during your lifetime in the event of your incapacitation and after your death. Although both these documents provide similar ends, the liv-ing trust is a way of transferring assets while you are alive and of avoiding probate court after you die.

There are several types of living trusts and wills, and it is prudent to consult with a lawyer to review your personal sit-uation and make the best choices possible.

However, there are self-help sources available on the Web and at your local computer software store. I advise you to see a lawyer to prepare your will or living trust, but a do-it-yourself version is better than none at all. Try for additional self-help information.

As you write up your will, you will have to think through many scenarios and name certain people to special roles. One of these roles is called *executor*, and this is the person who will be responsible for settling your estate. Your choice of an executor is very important because this person will be carrying out your personal wishes.

You also will need to name beneficiaries who will be the recipients of your assets.

If you go through a divorce or major life change, the wishes you express in your will may change dramatically, so it is important to revise your will immediately following any significant life event. It's also important to review your will as your kids grow up and their needs change.

Drawing up a will is part of what a financially healthy person does. I don't know if people with wills live longer, but I suspect that they live more peacefully knowing that their exact wishes will be carried out once life is over.

Death and taxes and childbirth! There's never any convenient time for any of them.

Scarlett O'Hara

25

▶▶▶▶ DON'T ◀◀◀◀
worry about
money

Think I'm kidding? Well, I'm not. After all, it is just money—and not your health, your love life, your children's well-being, or anything of eternal value.

So keep money in perspective. It's a tool. A tool that can be used properly or improperly. A tool that can enhance the important things in your life or deplete you of the energy to enjoy what is truly meaningful.

More of it won't change your life, and less of it won't destroy you. However, ignoring the reality of money is as futile as ignoring our bodies' need for food and water. You can just ignore it for so long.

And women, as a group, have been ignoring money for too long. Perhaps it's just another way that we take care of everybody and everything but ourselves. Perhaps it's all the Cinderella messages we received as children. Perhaps it's just not wanting to make a fuss. Whatever it is, it's time to change.

We've come such a long way in so many areas—particularly in the professional fields—yet our level of financial literacy has not risen substantially in the last two decades. If we want to change, to lead truly whole and satisfying lives, then

we must be willing to accept the challenge of personal financial responsibility. And we must begin to teach our children,
particularly our daughters, the basics of money management.

Wherever you are in the spectrum of life, it's not too late
or too early to start building your financial health. The results
not only will be a bigger bank account but, more importantly, a fuller, more peaceful, and complete life. A life you'll be
proud to call your own.

Start now.

*There must be more to life than having
everything.*

MAURICE SENDAK

DOs

AND

DON'Ts

The Gray Areas of
Your Money Life

Not everything in life is a black and white, do-or-die decision. In fact, some of the decisions you make daily are quite subjective. Yet you probably make these choices—whether big or small—effortlessly, relying on your instincts, your life experience, and the counsel of friends.

The same holds true with your financial life.

While there are many "absolute money truths" that have been explained in this book, there are also many gray areas that you must approach intelligently by evaluating both the pros and cons of the issue at hand.

In short, there's not an easy answer for every financial question. Some questions require a judgment call. Here are some frequently debated (and misunderstood) issues.

1. SHOULD YOU BUY OR RENT YOUR HOME?

Typical financial dogma stipulates that buying is always better than renting. But that's not always the case.

Sure, if you are flush with cash for a down payment and if you are staying put at one address for more than a few years, it's smart to buy for an obvious reason: When you buy you're putting your money toward a purchase so that you will have equity (your money invested) to regain when/if you sell your home. In addition, if you stay in your home until it is paid for, then you will never have to pay rent again.

But there are reasons to rent, at least during certain periods of your life. For example, if you are in the midst of a life change such as a career move or a divorce, it probably makes sense to rent so that you retain the flexibility to adjust to unforeseen changes. It also makes sense to rent if you intend to move within a few years; a home investment does not generally produce a short-term financial gain, and the costs to buy and sell may exceed any increase in the value of your home if you have to sell quickly.

It's smart to rent if you see housing prices fall, as this affords you the opportunity of waiting and getting a better deal. You certainly don't want to buy a home at top market prices—it's better to wait for a "sale" just as you would wait for a discount on expensive clothing.

Finally, it's wise to look at home buying as an investment—but an investment that can rise or fall according to many factors that are out of your control, just as the stock market is out of your control. If you invest in a home (via your down payment and monthly payments), you have the benefit of living in your investment and knowing that your monthly mortgage is really a forced investment strategy. However, if you rent instead, you have the money you would otherwise have used for your down payment, mortgage interest, and maintenance to put into other investments that may yield a higher return (profit over time) than a house.

Confused?

Here are some bottom line considerations:

- *Rent* if you are in a period of transition, are unsure of how long you will stay in one place, or are in a geographic location where housing prices are falling.
- *Buy* if you want to stay in the house for more than a few years, if you are in a market where housing prices are increasing, or if you are not disciplined enough to invest the money you would use for a down payment.

Although there has been a great deal of talk about falling housing prices and a bursting housing bubble, the truth is that over the last 15 years there has not been a decline in home prices in most large metropolitan areas.[1] Therefore, home buying is generally viewed as a safe investment.

2. SHOULD YOU GO FOR A HIGHER SALARY OR A SANER LIFE?

This question may imply that a high salary and a sane life are mutually exclusive, but that is not true. What is true is that there are often tradeoffs between big bucks and quality of life issues—and that balance is generally the goal.

If you are struggling to find that balance for yourself, first realize that there are no perfect answers. There will be periods in your life when you will have the time and flexibility to super-charge your career, and there will be periods when work just doesn't work anymore.

Let's look at some hypotheticals.

Perhaps you are in your thirties and have a promising career, a new baby, and a toddler. What do you do? Well, again there is no easy answer. But it is possible to apply a bit of financial reality to this otherwise emotionally driven life period.

Start by writing down everything you do at home, and, realistically, what it would cost to hire replacement services. Consider not just child care but also housekeeping services, errand-running, and transportation. Add up the cost of these services for a year and then multiply the sum by three. If your salary does not equal or exceed this amount, if you are not the sole financial provider for your family, and if you have the desire to stay at home with your kids, then consider leaving the professional world for a few years. From a financial point of view, you are not getting ahead unless you can earn (before taxes) three times the cost of replacing yourself at home.

Now what if you are making a mid-life change in professions? Does it ever make sense to forego money for something else you desire: time off, involvement in the community, indulging in the arts?

The answer is, emphatically, yes.

Evaluate your options with a clear head by writing down your thoughts. Make a list of what you want to achieve and how you will do it. Most importantly, think clearly about your financial life. Is it possible to streamline your personal spending so that you can afford this change? Are there other options—such as staying in your existing job but negotiating to work fewer hours so that you have time for your other pursuits?

There are most likely many ways to achieve both your financial goals and your personal dreams. If you find that you cannot afford to make a career change right now—that you cannot streamline your life to allow a change—then don't consider your dream a dead issue. Write down what you want to achieve and exactly how and when you intend to accomplish it.

Most of all, realize that you do have choices and that the decisions you make at one point in your life may not be right for another time in your life. Think outside the parameters of the typical. Decide what you want and ask for it. You may be surprised at how receptive your employer/partner/spouse is when you express your goals in a clear and objective way.

3. SHOULD YOU GET A HOME EQUITY LOAN OR BORROW MONEY A DIFFERENT WAY?

If you need money to pay for life expenses that are critical and cannot wait, such as medical care or education, it may make sense to consider a home equity loan rather than borrow money through other ways.

Since Texas voters recently approved a constitutional amendment allowing lines of credit backed by home equity, residents in all 50 states can now take advantage of this type of lending. But is it smart to get a home equity loan? Sometimes it is and sometimes it isn't. Let's look.

First, it's important to understand what a home equity loan is. Briefly, a home equity loan is a loan that a financial institution makes based upon the amount of equity—or hard dollars—that you have in your home. Financial institutions are comfortable with this type of loan because it is safe for them. There are terms for the payback, such as a set interest rate and monthly payments. If you cannot meet these terms, the financial institution is still assured that it will be repaid because it can force the sale of your home in order to receive repayment. (The same is *not* true for unsecured loans such as credit cards. You can walk away from this debt, even though it may scar your credit report and cause you a great deal of grief.)

Home equity loans have increased in popularity due to the impressive appreciation (growth) of real estate prices in the last decade, low home mortgage interest rates, and high consumer debt.

More of us now own homes and have financed them at low interest rates, resulting in an increase in the dollar value of our homes. In fact home equity climbed about $405 billion in 2001–2002—at the same time that stock portfolios decreased about $1.4 trillion.[2] Yet more of us also have credit card and other high-interest debt. That's why home equity loans are popular.

Let's say that you need to borrow $10,000. You can access this amount on a credit card and pay perhaps 15 percent or more in interest fees.

The advantages of borrowing on a credit card are that it is easy, immediate, and doesn't cause you to "pledge" anything else that you own. In addition, if you are in a cash-poor situation, you can make minimum payments, which cover interest primarily, until you have the funds to start paying back the real debt.

The disadvantages are that you are paying a very high interest rate and that you may be tempted to delay paying back the real debt (called principal). As a result, you may end up in credit-card "jail," because you will keep accruing interest while you are making minimum payments.

On the other hand, a home equity loan will allow you to borrow money at a much lower interest rate. This makes sense as long as you do not fall into the trap of using your home as a credit card or ATM.

Why is this a danger? Because owning your home outright may be the most important financial move you ever make. It is an important step toward financial freedom. If you choose to borrow against the value of your home, do so with care. You do not want to meet short-term financial goals by jeopardizing your long-term financial health.

Heaven forbid, you also do not want to risk being forced to sell your home in order to pay off a debt. This is called foreclosure. Although foreclosures are now at a record high, they still occur infrequently—under 2 percent for conventional loans.[3] Still, foreclosures happen, and you don't want one to happen to you.

Bottom line? If you need to borrow money and are considering a home equity loan, make sure that you are borrowing for something that is important enough to put the owner-ship of your home at risk. In some cases it may be. However, *never* use a home equity loan as a means of paying everyday expenses. A home equity loan may seem like easy money, but it will devastate you in the long run if used in this way. Do everything else, like taking a second job and slicing your expenses, first.

4. SHOULD YOU START YOUR OWN BUSINESS OR STICK WITH YOUR JOB?

I see countless women who dream of starting their own busi-nesses yet wonder if and how they can make it financially. Generally, these women are motivated by the desire to seek balance and to reap the rewards of their own hard work—building up assets for their futures and not their employers' success.

But the question of entrepreneurship versus employment is complicated. And timing is critical. The decision is like the decision of buying or renting a home and may depend heav-ily upon your stage of life.

For starters, look at these statistics. In 1998, women-headed households with a business had an average income level of 2.5 times that of those without a business and an aver-age net worth of 6 times those without.[4] Additionally, in 1998, of all U.S. sole proprietorships, 37 percent were operated by women, and women-owned businesses generated 22 percent of total business net income.[5] So women are starting busi-nesses and running them successfully.

But is entrepreneurship right for you?

Start by asking yourself these questions: What do I want to achieve by starting my own business? How much money do I *have* to earn to cover life's basic expenses? And how will I handle the business of running my business (things like tax forms, payroll, and accounting)?

When you are employed, it is easy to look at your employer and imagine that he or she is personally benefiting from all the income you are generating from your hard work. But that may or may not be the case. What you often don't see behind the scenes is the reality that the company for which you work may be sending out invoices and waiting 60 to 90 days to receive payments from clients, making it impossible for the business owners to take a steady salary. You probably also are not aware of the myriad tax forms and paperwork required by local, state, and federal governments.

I am not trying to talk you out of starting your own business, as it is immensely rewarding to do so. But I am trying to shine light on the reality that starting a business is harder than it seems. In fact, I am reminded of a running joke I have with my friends: Sure, when you have your own business you can work any hours you want to—as long as the hours are 24/7.

So make sure you have the passion and staying power to last through hard times if you decide to start a business. It will be important for you to have some savings stashed away so that you can make it through down times without adding up credit card or other debt.

If you do decide to go for business ownership, look for smart sources of funding your dreams. Although women are starting businesses in record numbers, they are not seeking and taking advantage of the funds and programs that are available to them. In fact, in 2000, women-owned businesses were granted only $4.6 billion in federal prime contracts, a mere 2.3 percent of total federal procurement.[6] And the total share of SBA (Small Business Administration) loans issued to women-owned businesses dropped to 21 percent in 2000 from a high of 24 percent in 1995.[7]

Starting your own business is very exciting and just might be the path you need to take in order to maximize your earning power while building the balanced and healthy life you want to lead. So—go for it if it's in your heart to join the ranks of female entrepreneurs. But go for it with your head as well as your heart.

5. SHOULD YOU HIRE A FINANCIAL PLANNER OR DO THE PLANNING YOURSELF?

Today there are many resources to help you with your financial life, and hiring a planner or advisor may be the right move for you. However, there are pros and cons to hiring a planner, so it's best to do some research and soul-searching before you spend time and money for professional counsel.

Hiring a financial advisor is a great move if you are "stuck" in your financial life, just beginning to strategize financially, or are in a particularly complex situation. Otherwise, the services that planners provide are services that you can provide for yourself, given that you have the time and interest to do so.

How can a financial advisor assist you? Well, first of all, an advisor can help you sort out objectives and solidify a workable financial strategy no matter what stage of life you are in. If you are new to financial planning, then it's a good idea to work with a professional so that you have solid counsel and a sounding board as you look to the future.

In particular, a planner or advisor can help you avoid the common mistakes that novices make. Often a planner can help you "get off dead center" and get moving with a plan because you have the motivation of reporting to the planner— just as you reported to your teachers when you were in school. Additionally, a planner can help you react in an objective manner to short-term market fluctuations and investment decisions—so you won't rely exclusively on your emotions when making decisions.

There is an inherent discipline involved in working with a planner, as you have dates and checkpoints, and these are helpful deadlines for anyone. If you want to be as buttoned-up as possible, then a planner is important because he or she can help you make sure all of the i's are dotted and the t's are crossed in your financial life. Finally, it's important to work with a planner if you just hate to handle your financial life on your own. You don't have to excel in everything, and it may be that relying on someone else for financial counsel will be the smartest move you could make, allowing you more time to focus on your own talents and expertise.

But . . . there is a flip side to this decision.

Many women with whom I've spoken have told me that they have been embarrassed to tell all to their financial advisors. And many financial advisors have told me that their clients have neglected to tell them important facts about their financial life. The results are disastrous. So, if you are not willing to tell your financial planner *everything* that relates to your financial life, don't hire one. It will be a waste of money.

That's why for some people, particularly "do-it-yourselfers," taking on a financial plan for yourself is probably a good idea. Certainly it is wise if you have the self-motivation and discipline to carry it off. Plus you will save the fees related to hiring a financial planner—and, no matter *how* the relationship is structured, you will pay a fee for professional help.

How do financial planners charge? Many are commission-based, so they do not charge a visible fee to develop a plan but are compensated when you buy stocks, bonds, mutual funds, or other financial products based upon their recommendations. While this type of planner may be exactly suited to your needs, it is important to realize that there may be a hidden agenda to the plan, since the planner makes money only if you make purchases.

Other planners work on a fee basis, which may be a percentage based upon the value of your account, a flat monthly fee, or an annual charge. Fee-based planning is increasingly popular because it allows you, the client, to know up front exactly how and what you are paying for.

Whatever your decision—to use a planner or go on your own—it's important that you stay involved with the process and understand what's happening with your money. If you invest in a mutual fund, bond, or stock, try to learn as much as possible about the company's performance. The final decision is always yours.

6. SHOULD YOU PAY WITH CASH OR CREDIT?

It may seem odd to bring up the subject of paying with credit rather than cash after all of the admonitions in this book about credit-card debt. But, in reality, credit is not all bad. It's how you use it—and whether it is in control of you or you are in control of it—that matters.

The biggest factor in determining whether or not you should pay for items in cash or credit is your own self-awareness and discipline. In fact, this may be the only factor. That's because lines of credit, credit cards, and loans on large purchases such as cars make a lot of financial sense—if they are not overused.

In our current economy interest rates are very low, so it is possible to get attractive lending rates on major purchases and on credit cards—rates that make it economically viable for you to pay with plastic and save your money. In this scenario, you have the added benefit of "float," which is the ability to operate with someone else's money while you are investing your own.

How does float work? Well, imagine that you are buying expensive airline tickets for an upcoming trip. If you make the purchase via a credit card, you will retain your cash for 30 days, so you have more money to invest in interest-producing entities. In essence, you are buying tickets with the credit-card company's money. This is a smart strategy as long as you remember to pay your credit-card bill on time and you resist the temptation to use the float for other expenditures. The problem comes if and when you don't plan for the payment that will be due in 30 days. Then it is easy to fall into the trap of minimum payments, which means that it could take years to pay off a modest sum, because interest keeps adding up on the principal and interest.

Even though there are advantages to the strategic use of credit, it is more important to avoid credit at all costs if you are not able to budget your money and pay your credit card off fully at least most of the time. Use the minimum payments for emergencies only and carefully watch when payments are due. Even being 1 day late can put you on the "over 30 day" list and damage your credit rating.

It is important to establish credit, so be judicious if you are starting out or making a life change. As discussed in detail elsewhere in this book, your credit report is important and will follow you in almost every area of your life.

So handle your credit with as much care as your cash.

7. SHOULD YOU INVEST IN MORE EDUCATION OR LEAVE WELL ENOUGH ALONE?

If you are in college now, take this advice and get as much education as time and money allow.

End of story.

But if you are in the midst of your career and wondering if you should improve your résumé by adding more credentials, read on.

Reinventing is the new corporate trend.

The professional world today is moving at an unbelievably fast pace. Even the page I am writing now will be somewhat outdated by the time you read these words. No one can keep up completely. But your chances of staying current and on top of your professional game increase if you make it a point to keep up your credentials.

Still, is it cost-effective to go back to school for that executive MBA program with a price tag of $40,000 and up? It may or may not be, but it is worth considering this and other options to assist with your personal reinvention, if that is your objective.

If you are in a rapidly changing field such as high-tech, it may be mandatory to invest in more education. Even if you are in a traditional field, it may be important to your career to receive additional credentials. Certainly if you are contemplating a major career move or planning to start a business, it will be important to seek knowledge about general business practices. But strategize carefully first in order to maximize your future financial rewards. Don't just jump into school and assume that you will immediately increase your earning power. Some employers don't care about your education after you are a part of the company and performing well. Others are only impressed with degrees from the top-ranking schools. So find out what's going to make an impression.

Next check out possible employer contributions. Your employer may underwrite all or part of the cost of your tuition, books, and fees. But more often than not, you'll have to pay for this education yourself.

If you do decide to pursue additional education, then make sure you focus and spend your time and money where it counts. While there are certain careers that benefit from full-press degrees, many careers can be enhanced with just certificate courses from local universities. These are affordable night or weekend courses that often allow you to do a great deal of work on-line. Still, certificate courses look great on a résumé.

If you are paying personally for your certificate, seminar, or degree, talk with your CPA about whether or not you can deduct the cost of your education from your income tax. This can make a big year-end difference.

The decision whether or not to return to school can make a life-long difference.

8. SHOULD YOU CHOOSE LOVE OR MONEY?

Alas, the timeless question remains relevant today. But the question of love or money is not applicable just to the world of romance. It is also applicable to other life decisions and to your career.

It may seem impossible to approach the issue of love or money without emotion but that's exactly what you need to do: Look at your choices straight and clearly.

If you are in a relationship and contemplating marriage, this may seem heartless and cold, but the fact is that marriage is a partnership and a legal agreement. In fact, marriage is much more binding than most business arrangements, so it's not something to enter into without a clear understanding of financial expectations. Whether or not your marriage lasts, the financial ramifications will stay with you for a lifetime.

Prenuptial agreements are covered in this book and are highly recommended as a way to articulate and objectify the financial aspects of marriage. But before you even get to the prenup, you have to make a personal decision about what is important to you.

It takes money to live a certain lifestyle, yet that is a reality we sometimes overlook when we are involved in a romance. It is also a reality we sometimes overlook when planning our careers and other life decisions. Blind Love and Starving Artists were not accidentally named.

So am I recommending that you throw out your dreams and go for the hard cash?

No.

But I am recommending that you balance your heartfelt desires with some everyday practicality.

Before you make any important decision or enter into any relationship make sure that you understand the financial ramifications. It's good to start with where you are financially right now and where you want to be. Ask yourself if this situation or relationship will help you achieve your goals. Will it help you get where you want to be? If the answer is no, but your heart still says yes, then ask yourself if you can modify your goals to be more in keeping with the longings of your heart.

Bottom line, ask yourself if you are willing to cut back spending or work harder or do whatever it takes on the financial side to enable yourself to marry the guy with fewer financial assets or to pursue a not-so-lucrative career. Be honest with yourself now.

It is not wrong to decide that you really can't make the life adjustments to live on less income. So make that choice. It's also not wrong to decide that you can't live without following your heart regardless of the money. It's just a different choice.

What's wrong is not deciding. The lack of clarity will make it difficult to achieve either the love or the financial success you want.

Choose wisely.

Happiness depends,
as Nature shows,
less on exterior things than most suppose.

WILLIAM COWPER, TABLE TALK

Resources

CREDIT REPORTS

1. How to Check Your Credit Report

Each request costs approximately $8 and is done on an individual (not joint) basis—so you have to request separate reports for you and your spouse. Also be sure to ask for reports under different names if you have, for example, gone back and forth using your maiden and/or married names over the years. If you have been turned down for credit, you are eligible for a free report.

TransUnion LLC

Consumer Disclosure Center
P. O. Box 1000
Chester, PA 19022
800-888-4213
www.transunion.com

Experian

P. O. Box 9600
Allen, TX 75013
888-397-3742
www.experian.com

Equifax, Inc.

P. O. Box 740241
Atlanta, GA 30374
800-685-1111
www.equifax.com

INCLUDE THE FOLLOWING IN YOUR REQUEST:

- Full name (including Jr., Sr., etc.)
- Social Security Number

- Current and previous addresses within past 5 years
- Two proofs of address, such as a driver's license and a utility bill
- Date of birth
- Telephone number
- Signature

2. Other Important Information About Credit Reports

WHAT DO LENDERS LOOK FOR?

- A superior score (called a Beacon or FICO score) is between 720 and 850.
- A score of 660 and above is considered adequate.
- Below 620 means that you may be considered a higher risk and may be faced with a higher interest rate, a prepayment penalty, or extra points.
- Payment in full of a debt does *not* mean that the debt will be removed from your credit report. Here is the length of time that various debts will remain:
    - Bankruptcies (Chapters 7, 11, and nondischarged 13) will remain for 10 years from date filed.
    - Discharged Chapter 13 bankruptcies will remain for 7 years from date filed.
    - Paid tax liens will remain for 7 years.
    - Judgments will remain for 7 years.
    - Debts placed for collection after January 1, 1998, will remain for 7 years from the beginning of the delinquency.

3. How Are Credit Scores Used to Calculate Insurance Risk?

AUTO INSURANCE COMPANIES LOOK AT THESE FIVE MAIN FACTORS TO DETERMINE INSURANCE RATES:

- *Payment history.* This comprises 35 percent of your score.
- *Amount of debt.* This comprises 30 percent of your score.
- *Length of credit history.* This comprises 15 percent of your score.

- *New credit.* This comprises 10 percent of your score.
- *Types of credit in use.* This comprises 10 percent of your score.

4. What If You Divorce?

A divorce decree does not release you from legal responsibility on any account. It is your responsibility to contact each creditor and seek their legal, binding release.

5. What If You Have a Dispute?

You can dispute information by writing each credit bureau and providing proof of the error. If an error is found and verified, it must be removed from the file quickly, usually within 30 days.

For more details on your rights under the Fair Credit Reporting Act, go to www.ftc.gov. This site explains rights, which may vary from state to state.

HOW CREDIT CARDS HURT YOU

- An introductory annual percentage rate (APR) is just that—introductory. You have to read the fine print to see what you're interest rate will be after the brief, low-interest period.
- Most grace periods (where you can repay the debt without interest) are 25 days—not 30. And that means the credit-card company has to receive and process the payment within 25 days after the billing date, so you must make the payment even sooner.
- Your introductory rate will have a time limit. It also may be increased if you pay over 30 days late or exceed your credit limit.
- Credit-card companies generally will allow you to exceed your credit limit and will not give you a warning that this is happening. You will just find out after your interest rate increases.
- Your minimum payment will seem like a great idea because it is generally 3 percent of your balance, but if you only pay the minimum payment, it will take years to pay off the account, and you will spend enormous sums in interest. An example—if you make minimum payments of $10 per month on a $2500

balance, you will pay an additional $2224 in interest, and it
will take over 14 years to clear the balance.

- To see the best rates on credit cards, go to www.lendingtree.com
  or www.bankrate.com.

HOW TO KEEP TEMPTATION AT BAY

1. Opt Out of Credit-Card Solicitations

This takes your name off all mailing lists provided by the main consumer reporting agencies—TransUnion, Experian, and Equifax.

This is per person, not per family, so each family member needs
to opt out. Call 888-OPTOUT (888-567-8688) or write:

TransUnion LLC's Name Removal Option
P. O. Box 97328
Jackson, MS 39288-7328

INCLUDE

- First, middle, and last names (including Jr., Sr., III, etc.)
- Current address
- Previous address (if current address is newer than 6 months)
- Social Security Number
- Date of birth
- Signature

2. Opt Out of Phone Solicitations

WRITE TO

Direct Marketing Association
Telephone Preference Service
P. O. Box 9014
Farmingdale, NY 11735-9014

INCLUDE

- First, middle, and last names (including Jr., Sr., III, etc.)
- Current address
- Home area code and phone number

3. Opt Out of Mailing Lists (for Catalogs, etc.)

WRITE TO

Direct Marketing Association

Mail Preference Service
P. O. Box 9008
Farmingdale, NY 11735

INCLUDE

- First, middle, and last names (including Jr., Sr., III, etc.)
- Current address

HOW COMPOUND INTEREST WORKS MAGIC FOR YOU

Compound interest is important because it is a way of making money without working; your money does the work for you.

Compound interest works because you make interest on the interest. If you grasp this concept, you'll be way ahead.

Here's an example that shows the merits of saving early: Person A begins saving at age 21 and saves $100 per month every month until she is 31. At that point she has invested $12,000 (this does not include interest earned), and then she lets the money sit in an account until she is 65. Person B begins saving at age 35 and also saves $100 per month but saves monthly until she is 65. At that point she has invested $36,000.

Who has more money for retirement? Common sense would say that Person B has more because she has saved more. But the reality is that Person A has much more money, even though she saved $24,000 less.

If we assume an annual interest rate of 8 percent, compounded monthly, Person A ends up with $300,053, whereas Person B has only $150,030.

Feel like you got left out? Here's an example to help your kids or grandkids: When your baby is born, save $100 per month in an investment account from ages 0 to 6. If you never touch the money and it earns 8 percent, your child will have will be a millionaire at age 65, with $1,107,869. And all you invested was $7,200.

KEY FINANCIAL TERMS EXPLAINED

401(k)—A program offered by many employers that allows you to save for retirement using pretax dollars. The company managing your 401(k) invests the money in bonds, mutual funds, or the company's own stock.

Bear market—A period of time when stock prices in general are declining.

Blue-chip stock—These are stocks issued by very established companies, so they are considered to be great investments. The name *blue chip* comes from the blue poker chip, which is the most valuable.

Bond—An IOU issued by a business or a government. The entity issuing the bond pays you back and pays interest, which is how you make money. There are various types of bonds—some safer investments than others.

Broker—Someone who sells financial products such as stocks and insurance. Most are compensated by a percentage of what they sell to you. Some may charge a flat fee.

Bull market—A period of time when stock prices are in general increasing.

Certificate of deposit (CD)—A type of savings account offered by many banks. It pays interest to you but requires you to keep your money in the account for a period of time.

Diversification—This is a strategy of investing that means not having all your eggs in one basket. This is considered good.

Dividend—A payment to shareholders from earnings of a stock. Not all stocks pay dividends.

Dividend reinvestment plan—A plan that lets investors automatically reinvest stock dividends into additional stock.

Dollar cost averaging—This means regularly putting equal amounts of money into an investment in order to allow you to buy more shares when a stock is low and less when it is high.

Dow Jones Industrial Average—The oldest index of the stock market. The Dow represents the average of 30 important American companies, so it is used as an indicator of how the stock market is doing.

Federal Reserve—This is the central bank of the United States and oversees interest rates and credit and money supplies.

Index—A group of securities that you can buy as a "mix" of individual stocks. The performances of the indexes is generally used to judge the stock market overall. Major indexes include the Dow Jones Industrial Average and the Standard and Poor's 500.

IRA—This means Individual Retirement Account and is a type of savings that allows you to put away money before it is taxed. The financial institution where you put the money may invest it in different types of securities.

Keogh—A tax-deferred retirement savings plan for self-employed people. There are other plans for self-employed people, but the Keogh is common.

Margin account—A scary way to buy stock. This type of account allows you to borrow money from your broker in order to buy stock, but if the stock values go down, you have to pay the difference.

Mutual fund—An investment company that will invest your money in a diversified way, which the company explains in a prospectus. Putting money into a mutual fund is considered safer than buying individual stocks because the risk is lowered due to the mix of companies in the fund.

NASDAQ—Began as the world's first electronic stock market and today is where many high-tech stocks are traded.

New York Stock Exchange—The oldest stock exchange in the United States. It is the exchange that you see in movies where ticker tape is everywhere and is located on Wall Street.

P/E ratio—This is the share price of a stock divided by its earnings per share over the last year and is used as an indicator of how the stock is doing.

Portfolio—A way of referring to all the holdings (securities and stocks) of an individual or institution.

Roth IRA—A type of retirement account where contributions are not tax-deductible but withdrawals at retirement are.

SEC—Security and Exchange Commission—this is the federal agency that is responsible for ensuring that the U.S. stock market is operated as a free and open market.

Security—A confusing use of a common word. Here it means a stock or financial asset that can be traded.

Standard & Poor's 500—This is an index (like the Dow Jones) that is used as a barometer of how the overall stock market is doing. The S&P 500 is composed of 500 of the biggest publicly traded companies in the United States. If you buy a part of the S&P (which you can do—just like a stock), then the shares are sometimes called spiders.

Stock—An ownership share in a corporation that allows you to share in the company's successes and failures.

Ticker symbol—An abbreviation for a company's name that is used as a "quick read." The trick is that the ticker symbol does not always correspond with the company's initials. For example, Coca-Cola's ticker symbol is KO.

Volatility—The amount of ups and downs in the stock market.

Endnotes

DOs

1. Women's Financial Network, wwwWFN.com, 2001.
2. Women's Financial Network, www WFN.com, 2001.
3. Employee Benefit Research Institute, Retirement Confidence Survey, Washington, DC 2002.
4. National Center for Women and Retirement Research, Long Island University Southampton College, 2001.
5. Women's Institute for Financial Education, San Diego, CA 2003.
6. Study by economists at the University of California at Davis, as quoted in *Individual Investor*, February 2000.
7. National Center for Health Statistics: "First Marriage Dissolution, Divorce and Remarriage: U.S. Advance Data 323," Hyattsville, MD 2002.
8. McNeil, John M. 2001. "Americans with Disabilities: Household Economics Studies." U.S. Bureau of the Census. Current Population Reports, U.S. Government Printing Office, Washington DC 2001, pgs 70–73.
9. The Hartford Financial Services Group, Inc., *PR Newswire*, Simsbury CT, April 2003.
10. The Hartford Financial Services Group, Inc., *PR Newswire*, Simsbury CT, April 2003.
11. National Center for Women and Retirement Research, Long Island University Southampton College, 2000.
12. Odean, Terrance, and Brad Barber. "Boys Will Be Boys: Gender, Overconfidence and Common Stock Investment." *Quarterly Journal of Economics*, Feb. 2001, VOL 116, 1, pgs. 261–292.
13. Hira, Tahira K., and Olive Magenda. "Gender Differences in Financial Perceptions, Behaviors and Satisfaction." *Journal of Financial Planning*. Table No. 3, Article 11, Feb. 2000.

14. "Nellie May Summary Statistics College Credit Card Usage 2001," Braintree, MA 2002.

15. "Nellie May Summary Statistics College Credit Card Usage 2001," Braintree, MA 2002.

16. "Nellie May Summary Statistics College Credit Card Usage 2001," Braintree, MA 2002.

17. Washington (AP) March 2001 amendment proposed by Dianne Feinstein, D-CA.

18. U.S. Chamber of Commerce, 2003 as quoted in *The New York Times*, March 19, 2003.

19. Simon, Ruth, and Christine Whelan. *Wall Street Journal*, Sept. 3, 2002, pg D1.

20. "Nellie May Summary Statistics College Credit Card Usage 2001," Braintree, MA 2002.

21. Women's Institute for Financial Education, San Diego CA 2003.

22. "The Funds, Friends and Faith of Happy People," *American Psychologist* Vol. 55, No. 1, published by the American Psychology Association.

DON'Ts

1. Knuckey, Deborah. *Conscious Spending for Couples.* Hoboken, NJ: John Wiley & Sons, 2003.

2. National Center for Health Statistics: "First Marriage Dissolution, Divorce and Remarriage: U.S. Advance Data 323," Hyattsville, MD 2002.

3. Women's Financial Network, wwwWFN.com, 2001.

4. Bach, David. *Smart Women Finish Rich.* New York: Broadway Books, 2002.

5. Chatzky, Jean Sherman. Study. *Oppenheimer Funds & Money Magazine*, May 13, 2002.

6. Joint Center for Housing Studies, *State of the Nation's Housing.* Cambridge, MA: Harvard University, 2003.

7. "The State of the Nation's Housing: 2003, Housing and The Economy / Cash-Out Refinances Have Shattered All Records"

Joint Center for Housing Studies of Harvard University, Report. FIG # 7, pg 10, Source: Freddie Mac.

8. Tyre, Peg, and Daniel McGinn. "She Works, He Doesn't." *Newsweek* magazine, msnbc.com, May 12, 2003.

9. "Completing the Picture," Center for Women's Business Research, 2003, and "Women Entrepreneurs in the Equity Capital Markets: The New Frontier," National Foundation for Women Business Owners and Wells Fargo 2000 Study, Washington DC—study underwritten by Pitney Bowles Inc., the Philadelphia chapter of the National Association of Women Business Owners and WELLS FARGO.

10. Study by economists at the University of California at Davis, as quoted in *Individual Investor*, February 2000.

11. Employee Benefit Research Institute, Women's Retirement Conference Survey, 1999.

12. The Institute for Certified Divorce Planners, Southfield MI as referenced in the *Dallas Morning News*, Oct. 13, 1999, Helen Bond.

13. National Center for Women and Retirement Research, Long Island University Southampton College, 2001.

14. "Women Still Have Less Money for Retirement than Men," Women's Institute for a Secure Retirement, Washington DC, May 22, 2002.

15. www.nolo.com/lawcenter, 2003, Berkeley, CA.

DOs AND DON'Ts

1. Joint Center for Housing Studies, *State of the Nation's Housing*, Cambridge, MA: Harvard University, 2003.

2. Ibid.

3. Ibid.

4. U.S. Small Business Administration's Office of Advocacy, the Office of Economic Research, *Women in Business, 2001*, Washington, D.C.

5. Ibid.

6. Ibid.

7. Ibid.

Index

INDEX ◀ ◀ ◀ ◀ ◀ ◀ ◀ ◀ ◀ ◀ ◀ ◀ ◀ ◀ ◀ ◀ ◀ ◀ ◀

About the Author

Susan Jones is a marketing executive who has developed branding and positioning campaigns for companies such as Prudential Healthcare, ExxonMobil, and AMR Services. Her career has taken her from the position of copywriter to creative director and ad agency president over a 25-year span.

In addition to her award-winning work for national companies, Susan has worked as both a professional and a volunteer for social causes, including many nonprofits that directly benefit women. Currently, Susan is chief creative strategist for an advertising firm in Dallas, Texas.

Susan is a magna cum laude graduate of the University of Texas at Austin. She resides in Dallas, Texas, with her two teenage daughters and her cat, MaryAnne.